Susan U. Neal, MBA, MHS

"I love Susan Neal's bookselling plan and wholeheartedly recommend it—because it works. Her step-by-step system is clear, effective, and refreshingly doable, empowering authors to reach more readers without the usual overwhelm. If you're serious about book marketing, Susan's How to Sell 1,000 Books a Month is an essential addition to your author toolkit."
~**Linda Evans Shepherd**, bestselling author and founder of the Advanced Writers & Speakers Association

"Marketing your book doesn't have to be a nightmare! Susan Neal's *How to Sell 1000 Books a Month* proves the dreams of writers can come true. Her attention to detail and the step-by-step processes she supplies for writing and editing, proper use of SEO, finding beta readers, how to experience a successful book launch, and so much more helps us approach the act of selling as though we are simply breathing. This is a must buy for every published author."
~**Linda Goldfarb**, award-winning author, podcaster, and board-certified Christian life coach

"Every author wants to get their message into more hands—but most have no idea how. In *How to Sell 1,000 Books a Month*, Susan Neal offers a clear, practical roadmap to help Christian authors sell more books. This isn't theory—it is a tested, doable strategy from someone who's walked the path and generously shares the way. Highly recommended!"
~**Robyn Dykstra**, best-selling author and creator of Christian Speakers Boot Camp

"*How to Sell 1000 Books a Month* is packed with practical tips and forward-moving steps to succeed as an author. Writing from experience, author Susan Neal shares proven strategies in this concise guide that is a must-have for authors who are serious about their business."

~**PeggySue Wells**, award-winning and bestselling author of 45 titles including The Patent and The Ten Best Decisions a Single Mom Can Make

"*How to Sell 1000 Books a Month* serves as a comprehensive resource for author success. The book covers the full spectrum of publishing, including craft, marketing, publicity, and platform building. Detailed steps guide writers from basic thresholds to advanced levels for each part of the journey. Readers gain access to valuable resources and ongoing support. Susan Neal shares from her experience as an author who earns high-volume sales and as an industry executive who owns Christian Indie Publishing Association. Neal's book belongs on every writer's shelf."

~**Tina Yeager**, LMHC, Flourish-Meant media host, author, purpose coach, and publicity specialist

"Whether you're a novice or an established writer, you can shave years off your learning curve with Susan Neal's latest book, *How to Sell 1,000 Books a Month*. Susan knows how because she's done it herself. This comprehensive guide is full of valuable resources. It includes basic to advanced strategies, explaining not just the "what" but the "how." Do you need to know how to create your Media Kit, marketing plan, become a guest blogger, or create additional revenue streams? The pros and cons between traditional publishing vs self-publishing? Find all that and more here. You'll enjoy greater success after reading and applying the contents of this book. Let Susan guide you step-by-step, right in the comfort of your own home."

~**Patricia Durgin**, marketing and strategy coach at Marketers On A Mission

How to Sell 1,000 Books a Month

Strategies to Improve Sales

Susan U. Neal RN, MBA, MHS

CHRISTIAN INDIE
PUBLISHING

Copyright © 2025 by Susan U. Neal

Published by Christian Indie Publishing, LLC, 5568 Woodbine Road #89, Pace, FL. 32571

www.ChristianPublishers.net

All rights reserved. No part of this publication may be reproduced, stored in a retrieval system, or transmitted in any way or by any means—electronic, mechanical, recording, photocopy, or any other—except for brief quotations in printed reviews, without the prior permission of the publisher.

Scripture references marked NIV are taken from the Holy Bible, New International Version®, NIV® Copyright ©1973, 1978, 1984, 2011 by Biblica, Inc.® Used by permission. All rights reserved worldwide.

Scripture references marked NLT are taken from the *Holy Bible*, New Living Translation, copyright © 1996, 2004, 2015 by Tyndale House Foundation. Used by permission of Tyndale House Publishers, Inc., Carol Stream, Illinois 60188. All rights reserved.

All websites, programs, books, blogs, etc. in this book are offered as resources. They are not intended in any way to be or imply an endorsement by the author or publisher nor does the author or publisher vouch for the content of these resources for the life of this book.

Printed in the United States of America

ISBN: 978-1-7336443-3-4

Editor: Janis Whipple

Cover Design: Angie Alaya

Disclaimer and Terms of Use: Every effort has been made to ensure the information in this book is accurate and complete. However, the author and publisher do not warrant the accuracy or completeness of the material, text, and graphics contained in this book. The author and publisher do not hold any responsibility for errors, omissions, or contrary interpretation of the subject matter contained herein. This book is presented for motivational, educational, and informational purposes only. This book is sold with the understanding that the author and publisher are not engaged in rendering medical, legal, or other professional advice or services. Neither the publisher nor the author shall be liable for any damages arising herein, nor do they guarantee the author will sell 1000 books a month.

Contents

A Gift for You	vii
Introduction	ix
1. Map Your Literary Vision	1
2. Define Your Ministry and Audience	19
3. Build an Author Platform	39
4. Embark on the Journey of Newfound Knowledge	55
5. Master Search Engine Results through Blogging, Keywords, and Categories	69
6. Navigate the Publishing Journey: Traditional versus Self-Publishing	77
7. Plan a Successful Book Launch	95
8. Ignite Book Sales with Reviews	113
9. Amplify Book Visibility through Contests	123
10. Steps for Book Marketing	131
11. Increase Your Income Beyond Book Sales	147
12. Expand Your Reach through Advanced Marketing Strategies	167
Appendix 1: Author Resources	187
Appendix 2: Editorial Resources	191
Appendix 3: Certification Programs	193
About the Author	195
Other Products by Susan U. Neal	197

A Gift for You

I am excited you decided to take this divine-inspired journey into writing and publishing. As you progress through these chapters, you'll discover tasks to accomplish as you follow your dream of marketing your book. To streamline your efforts, I created a printable book marketing plan, available for download Sell1000BooksA-Month.com or SusanUNeal.com/marketing, to organize and implement your strategies effectively. I recommend printing this plan and completing it as you work through each chapter of this book.

For ongoing support and community, I invite you to join my exclusive Facebook group, How to Sell 1,000 Books a Month at SusanUNeal.com/1000 where I offer direct support, answer your questions, and foster a supportive community environment. You'll find a wealth of resources and media contacts shared within the group that can significantly aid your marketing efforts.

Additionally, the Christian Indie Publishing Association (CIPA) blog is another resource where I post articles, helpful tips, and updates at ChristianPublishers.net/blog. Subscribe to stay informed and well-equipped with the latest in book marketing and publishing.

Recognizing how crucial good health is for maintaining productivity, I've created the Healthy Living blog at SusanUNeal.com/HealthyLivingBlog. Here, you'll find tips and strategies to keep you at your best, physically and mentally, which is crucial for sustained creative output and productive energy.

For those who need more personalized guidance, my author coaching services are available at SusanUNeal.com/authorcoaching. Whether you're navigating the self-publishing process or looking to sharpen your marketing techniques, I'm here to assist you every step of the way.

This book and its accompanying resources will illuminate your career path as an author, ensuring you excel in the craft of writing and master the business side of publishing. Let's move forward together, equipped and inspired.

Introduction

Embarking on the journey to become a Christian author can be a daunting yet deeply rewarding experience. The path is filled with hopes and dreams, a calling to spread God's Word through our stories and teachings. However, the process is not without its challenges. Facing rejection from agents, publishers, and magazines can be disheartening, so it's essential to recognize this journey as a divine assignment from God.

As you navigate this complex vocation, it's natural to feel overwhelmed by the multitude of ideas and decisions about genres or themes that best suit your message. This book guides you through these uncertainties, offering direction and support as you explore the various facets of your calling. Starting with the basics, chapter 1 dives into writing styles, highlights the value of writer critique groups, and offers essential self-editing tips to refine your manuscript.

Chapter 2 helps you define your ministry and message and identify your target audience. It walks you through the practical aspects of creating a business plan and performing annual goal-setting. The journey begins when you identify your core values and build a following that resonates with them. If you're a seasoned author who has already published a book and established your mission statement, feel free to skip the first few introductory chapters.

The next stage is to build a robust author platform. Chapter 3 takes you through the stages of developing your online presence, from creating compelling lead magnets to designing email sequences that nurture your readers. The next chapter emphasizes the importance of gaining knowledge about the writing industry. One of the first steps is attending a writers' conference. Search engine optimization (SEO) is a vital part of our digital world, so chapter 5 teaches you how to become discoverable in a sea of online options. In chapter 6 you will learn the pros and cons of traditional versus self-publishing.

Book launches are a vital part of book marketing and chapter 7 shows you how—from securing endorsements to setting up a book launch. Part of a book's success comes from positive reviews, and chapter 8 shows you how to increase both reviews and sales. Having an award-winning book should be part of your book-marketing strategy, so chapter 9 teaches you how to obtain such recognition.

Once your book is published, marketing gets the book into the hands of your intended readers. Chapter 10 dives into the essential steps to market or sell your book, and how to use your unique personality traits to better connect with your audience. We all need to expand our income to support our ministry, and chapter 11 demonstrates how. The final chapter equips you with advanced marketing strategies to craft a personalized marketing plan and elevate your book sales. Some information may overlap between chapters because marketing is not necessarily a linear process. Don't let yourself get frustrated as you seek to learn, but focus on one task at a time.

This book is designed to guide your path—not only on the art of writing but also as a roadmap to the business of being a Christian author. You'll learn how to navigate the publishing world, sharpen your skills, and most important, how to touch more lives by selling more books. Remember, through God's guidance and the knowledge shared in these pages, your writing can become a powerful tool for spreading his love and wisdom. Let's embark on this journey together, with faith as our compass and God's wisdom as our map.

Chapter 1

Map Your Literary Vision

God has a unique way of whispering to our hearts the stories only we can tell—born from our deepest pains, triumphs, and lessons learned along life's winding road. Perhaps he's pressing upon you to share the raw honesty of a past trauma, the rich tapestry of generational tales, or the shadows of mental health struggles that have touched you and your family. It might even be the tender recounting of a loss that left a lasting mark on your soul. Each story is as unique as the person who writes it.

No matter what type of story God has called any of us to write, we have many different approaches to choose from when writing our stories. Authors often identify themselves as either plotters or pantsers terms that describe their approach to structuring a book. Plotters prefer to carefully outline their stories before they begin writing. As fiction writers they map out plot points, character arcs, and the novel's climax in advance, ensuring that the narrative flows smoothly and logically from start to finish. Nonfiction authors, like me, outline their chapters and the subjects or themes included in each one. This methodical approach can help a writer maintain focus and coherence.

On the other hand, pantsers write by the seat of their pants, meaning they dive into writing without a detailed plan and let the story develop organically. This grants a high degree of creativity and spontaneity as the story unfolds in unexpected ways based on the writer's moment-to-moment inspiration. This type of writing may require more revisions later.

Some writers find themselves somewhere in the middle, often referred to as plantsers, who combine both planning and spontaneity. They might outline major plot points but leave room for creative exploration as they write a novel. I am in this category, as my outlines for each chapter are minimal. As I write each chapter, I stick to the theme but allow the writing to develop as I go—then revise later. Understanding which style suits you best will enhance your writing process and help you tackle your projects more effectively.

However, no matter your style, I believe creating at least a minimal outline before beginning to write a book is crucial for several reasons. An outline serves as a roadmap, helping to structure your thoughts and ideas, ensuring that your book has a clear direction and logical flow. This prewriting step can significantly enhance your efficiency as it provides a framework you fill in with details as you write. It also helps maintain your message and thematic focus throughout your book, making it easier to keep track of character development, plot progression, and key themes.

Unlock Your Writing Potential

At times I've dictated three thousand words in one sitting. That's enough for a chapter. It is easy to sit down and tell your story and have your smartphone write the words for you. You can also use the dictation function on Microsoft Word under the Edit section. If you don't know where to begin in writing your book, use this method. Dictating is the simplest way I've found to write a book or an article. If you used your cell phone, transfer this text to your email, and then copy and paste it into your manuscript document.

Or perhaps putting actual pen to paper—or fingers to a keyboard—gets your creative juices flowing. So take that legal pad or laptop and start writing. Don't think of it as a blank page but as the opportunity to share what's on your heart and mind.

In either case, whether dictating or writing, don't start rattling off your story with no focus, which may end in a lot of wandering through the woods. Instead, follow your outline as you dictate to stay on the right path. Then let your story flow.

Initially you want to get the words written—the story told—without worrying about grammar or finding the perfect term. Writing engages the creative side of the brain. So let your story pour out of you without fixing misspellings or punctuation. After you compose your words, you can engage the analytical side of your brain to edit. If you try to edit while you write your story, your writing becomes stifled, and you get less written.

The right side of the brain, the creative side, needs room to flow. Find an inspirational environment. For me it is outside in nature. Maybe for you it is a specific room. Breathe deeply, pray, don't worry about anything. Focus on telling your story. Allow the details and insights about the experience or subject to flow freely from your mind without being concerned about phrasing.

Pretend your best friend is sitting with you as you share what is on your heart—what has been swirling in your mind for years. Write this portion of your story down before engaging the left side of your brain, which will evaluate and fix what you have written. (We'll cover self-editing in a later section.) Writing in this manner will prevent you from stumbling during the writing process.

The day after I write a portion of my book, I read what I wrote. I first read it through to remind myself of what I covered in that chapter or section. Reading aloud can also bring the content to light for you as you recall what you wrote. Then I engage my analytical brain to edit it. Reading and editing what's already written may shift me back into the writing frame of mind. So as I edit, I might add more to the story to explain it in more detail. I am usually surprised at how much more I will add. After editing what I wrote the previous day, I shift to use the creative side of my brain and write for several hours without editing.

I write best between 8:00 a.m. and 2:00 p.m., when I have the most energy and clarity of mind. You may be a night owl or an early bird. You might also have to work around your job hours or family times. Figure out what is the most productive time of day for you within your schedule, and write during that period. Make writing a priority and schedule it on your calendar.

I tell myself I can check my email or social media after 2:00 p.m. I especially like to write from 8 to 10 in the morning because I fast during this time and my body uses ketones for fuel versus glucose. This makes my mind clearer and more focused. Intermittent fasting works well for me. After dinner I eat nothing until the next morning around 10 a.m. It takes about twelve or more hours for the body to move from using glucose for energy to burning ketones.

Numerous scientific studies show that giving your body an extended break from digesting food comes with some incredible perks. Intermittent fasting helps a person lose weight (goodbye belly fat!), increase energy, balance blood sugar, and reduce inflammation. Fasting is part of my routine. If you would like to improve your diet and health, check out my assortment of books at SusanUNeal.com.

During my scheduled writing time, I do not divert my focus from writing. If I do, I lose my momentum. It takes fifteen minutes to get back into the writing mindset, so schedule your time, stick to it, and don't let anything interrupt you. I turn off my cell phone and the notifications on my computer.

My right brain seems to generate book ideas when I don't allow my left brain to dominate. When my mind is clear (of the busyness of the day), I am more apt to receive ideas to include in my book. When this occurs, I need to document those ideas, or I lose them. As I fall asleep, in the middle of the night, or when I am waking up, thoughts about what to add to my book surface. I keep a sheet of paper and pen in my bathroom so I can document ideas that come to my mind during these times. I always stop and write down these thoughts, because if I don't, in the morning they're gone. Find the best place for you to note ideas whenever they come—your phone, a notepad by your bed or favorite reading spot, wherever you can to capture those thoughts before they depart.

I also enjoy meditating, which activates the creative part of the brain. Calming my mind with meditation allows my creative juices to flow. Many studies have found that mediation enhances concentration and memory. We all need more of that. Why don't you try meditating with the Lord? Sit in a comfortable position and spend time with him as you read your devotion or Bible. At the end, meditate in his presence by closing your eyes and focusing on your breathing. Breathe deeply. Try not to think about anything and stay in that position until you feel ready to open your eyes.

During my meditation with the Lord, I'll have thoughts I never dreamed of before. This time provides an opportunity for my mind to stop spinning so I can focus on him. It is easier to hear God's still small voice during this quiet time. I keep a notepad and pen close by so I can jot down his divine thoughts that enter my mind during this time. I call these ideas "downloads from the Lord." They help me be a better person and give me deeper insight into my writing.

Gain Valuable Feedback

I highly recommend joining a Christian writers' group. I am in two Word Weaver groups (word-weavers.com), an international Christian writers' organization. Word Weavers International is dedicated to providing a forum for Christian writers to critique one another's work to improve each member's writing craft. Writers of all levels are welcome. It is inexpensive to join, and the groups meet monthly either in-person or online. Since this is a Christian group, you'll receive feedback on the spiritual content of your book and your writing. Some of my writer friends have experienced contrary and unhelpful feedback about the spiritual aspect of their prose at secular writing groups.

At a Word Weavers group, members bring a specific amount of writing to the meeting. A member of the group reads your piece aloud, so you will hear anything that doesn't sound accurate. Each member then critiques your submission. The group uses the sandwich method for the critique. The bread is encouragement, followed by the meat of the critique, and ends with more encouragement. By incorporating encouragement into the assessment, one can digest the critique without offense or feeling rejected.

Writers need to develop resilience and not feel insulted by someone's suggestion to enhance their writing. You do not have to incorporate everyone's recommendations. However, during each person's critique of your writing, you are not supposed to respond. You should listen and take in what they are saying without rebuttal. This technique prepares you for sitting in front of an editor or publisher at a writers' conference, who advises you regarding your writing. It's hard to do, but it is a great discipline to practice.

During your Christian writers' group, listen to members as they critique each other's work. You will learn much from them. I would not be where I am today in my writing career without my Christian critique groups. Sometimes, we can't see mistakes in our writing. An objective group can provide clarity. Constructive feedback improves our writing. It's also wonderful to gain confirmation on the spiritual content of our book from a faith-believing Christian.

Joining a writers' group provides accountability and motivation. Each month you've got to produce 1,500 words to submit for critique. Since I am in two groups, that's 3,000 words—a new book chapter each month. The group accountability provided the stimulus I needed to write my last book, *12 Ways to Age Gracefully: How to*

Look and Feel Younger. It took fifteen months, but without the motivation to submit my work monthly, I may not have completed it.

One time my group was reading the story of how I lost my health with ten medical diagnoses and two surgeries. I was going to place this story in an appendix in the back of my book. But my group advised putting the story in the first chapter because it was so gripping. I took their wise advice. It was the hook my book needed to peak the readers' interest. As Proverbs 27:17 shows, "As iron sharpens iron, so one person sharpens another" (NIV).

You'll likely become friends with members of your writing group. I drive seventy-five minutes one way each month to attend the meetings. Sometimes I spend the night at the founder's home because we have become close friends. Your family might not understand your writing life, but members of your writing group do. Being a Christian writer is an interesting career. We pour our hearts, souls, and money into this calling with not much of an earthly reward. We will receive our reward on the other side of eternity. Ultimately, we should be in this business to further the kingdom of God, not for earthly fame or fortune.

Self-Editing

Take the time to invest in your writing. As you read writing-craft books and learn from others in your writers' group, your writing and editing techniques advance. You will save a lot of money if you edit your book before submitting it to an editor. The fewer edits, the less time it takes for an editor to polish your prose. I apply the following tips for editing my manuscript.

Use an Online Manuscript Editor

I used Grammarly for years, but it is expensive. It catches mistakes I failed to recognize. Now I use ProWritingAid because if you purchase a lifetime subscription, it is much less expensive than Grammarly. (See appendix 1 for a list of author resource discounts.) ProWritingAid is a manuscript editing software that provides more features than most other similar software on the market. This program edits the grammar, spelling, and readability of your writing. Using a paid version of an online editor makes a significant difference in the professional appearance of your work. With each edit, you learn additional insights to further develop your writing craft.

Remove Weed Words
Each writer commonly develops the habit of repeating certain words or phrases. The pesky word that plagues my writing is the overuse of *important*. Instead, I have learned to use synonyms—vital, essential, or critical. Do an internet search for a weed word list. Many people use the same unnecessary terms frequently. You can find your weed words by carefully checking for these terms in your manuscript. Use the search or highlight features to show you how many times these words occur. Pull out those weed words and replace them with lively terms. As you participate in your critique group, others may help point out these undesirable words as well.

Use Active Voice and Vivid Verbs and Adjectives to Energize Your Writing
One critical area an online editing tool identifies is passive voice, offering suggestions to revise those sentences. With passive voice structure, the subject of the sentence is being acted upon rather than doing the action. (The dog is walked by her owner.) It can make writing feel stilted and awkward. Active voice begins with the subject. (The owner walks her dog.) Generally, passive voice is only

used when the object of the sentence needs to be emphasized. Active voice keeps your writing cleaner and tighter.

Passive voice often uses forms of *to be* verbs—was, were, are, is, had, have, or has. These common verbs drain energy from your prose. Replace them with stronger more descriptive verbs. Search lists of powerful verb options online to expand your vocabulary beyond the mundane overused passive verbs and use a thesaurus. Active terms like *sprinted* rather than *ran* inject movement into your writing. Active voice enlivens your prose and allows the reader to visualize the action.

Correct Common Misspelled Words

Even skilled writers often have a personal set of words that cause spelling mistakes. Spellcheck catches many errors, but some words evade detection. Be proactive and search for an online reference list of notoriously misspelled words to help prevent mistakes. As part of your self-editing, keep this list of tricky terms and check your manuscript for their spelling. Merriam-Webster's online dictionary also provides correct and preferred spelling and definitions of most terms. Here are a few to keep your eye on:

- accidentally or accidently
- affect or effect
- alright or all right
- altogether or all together
- although or though
- blonde or blond
- complement or compliment
- decent or descent
- doughnuts or donuts
- entitled or titled
- farther or further
- fewer or less

- foreword or forward
- historic or historical
- lightening or lightning
- it's or its
- loose or lose
- lying or laying
- OK or okay
- principle or principal
- then or than
- there, they're, or their
- who or whom
- who or that
- that or which
- your or you're

Vary Opening Words in Sentences, Paragraphs, and Chapters

Examine the first word of every paragraph throughout your manuscript. Avoid repeating the same introductory word, as this can feel monotonous for readers. Mix up those initial words.

Next, analyze the first word of every sentence within each paragraph. Just as you varied the paragraph openings, strive for diversity here as well, to prevent repetition of sentence starters. A mixture of structure and word choices avoids repetition and engages the interest of the reader.

Finally, review how each new chapter begins. Consider reworking repetitive chapter openings with a unique entrance into each chapter. Audit your opening words and sentence styles to inject more diversity into your writing rhythm. Polishing these details improves your style and reader enjoyment.

Verify Chapter Title Consistency

After you complete your manuscript, ensure the chapter titles in your manuscript match those in the table of contents. Print out the table of contents and crosscheck each individual chapter to validate the precise title to assure a match. Even minor discrepancies can compromise the integrity of your book. This careful process allows you to rectify any deviations. This is a vital step to delivering a polished manuscript.

Check for White Space

Check the length of your paragraphs throughout each chapter. Meticulously review each page of your manuscript, particularly for fiction works, to assess the balance of white space. Dense pages overwhelmed by lengthy, unbroken paragraphs can feel daunting to a reader. The page feels heavy, as opposed to the extra white space that naturally occurs when paragraphs are broken into shorter lengths along the way. If you find this issue in your manuscript, introduce more white space to enhance readability. Look for opportunities to divide longer paragraphs into two or three. This will alleviate the intimidating appearance of a large block of words and produce a more inviting layout. Ideally, you should do this as you go with each chapter you complete. But take the time to check again after the full draft is written. With strategic paragraph restructuring and white space allocation, your printed work evolves into a more aesthetically pleasing book. (For example, this paragraph was purposefully kept lengthy.)

Master the Hyphen, Em, and En Dashes

Within the realm of punctuation, dashes serve various roles, each with its own application. Hyphens unite compound words and phrases, seamlessly linking terms like *self-control* or *open-ended questions*. When used prudently, they facilitate clear and succinct communication.

The en dash, slightly longer than the hyphen, connects numerical ranges such as in "verses 1–2" or "pages 22–37." This structured difference is a writing element every writer should understand.

The em dash—the longest of the three—punctuates abrupt breaks in thought, similar to a comma but with greater dramatic impact. Em dashes can heighten a prose's rhythm—allowing writers to guide readers' focus with calculated interjections. An em dash can set off a phrase within a sentence and create a final thought or explanation at the end of a sentence.

Discerning the distinct roles of each dash and using them with precision elevates one's writing. Hyphens forge conceptual links, en dashes articulate numerical sequences, and em dashes strategically halt readers in their tracks—seamlessly integrating punctuation with the voice of the piece. Learning facets of grammar and punctuation is part of an author's compositional journey of writing.

Print Your Manuscript

Reading from a screen is much different than a printed page. Print your chapter or full manuscript so you can read it out loud. This is when you find awkward words that do not flow well. When you look at your book in a printed format, you'll notice how you can improve the text and white space. Read the text out loud or have Microsoft Word (or even a friend or writers' group member) read your text for you.

Editing from Others

Even the best writers never rely only upon their own eyes to judge the success of their writing. No matter how many times we read our own material, we will miss some things. Sometimes our own biases and blinders to our passionate message can keep us from an objective point of view. So once you have completed self-editing a portion or all of your work, engage the help of others. These should be people with some level of understanding and experience in either your subject, the craft of writing, or both.

I mentioned joining a Christian writers' group. Word Weavers is highly respected, but you may find others in your community. I've been a part of several groups for years, and some members have become my closest friends as they understand the writing life. Outside of this, here are a few other recommendations for editorial help.

Use Beta Readers

Beta readers are a group of people you enlist to give you feedback. They may be friends, fellow writers, or experts in your subject matter. One valuable way beta readers help an author is by notifying you of the errors they find. I suggest mailing a prepublication version of your printed book from kdp.com to your team members, or you could provide a portable document format (PDF) or an ebook file from BookFunnel.

I use BookFunnel because this platform sends a unique, nonsharable download link so only one person can open it, and you can check to see if they opened the file or not. Therefore, your manuscript cannot be shared with anyone else. (For a discount on BookFunnel, see appendix 1.)

Ask your beta team to text or email a photo of the mistakes they find in your manuscript. You might be surprised at how many they discover. Be sure to send them a gift for their hard work. For more information on using beta readers, see chapter 7.

Hire a Professional Editor

Every writer needs their manuscript edited by a developmental and copy editor. If you skip this step, you are omitting an essential ingredient of creating a professional-looking book. If your writing contains typos, inconsistencies, or other errors, your chances of success with book sales will be seriously affected. The people who buy your book may not read it all the way through, and probably won't recommend it to their friends. They might post negative reviews.

After you've written and edited part of your book and had the manuscript critiqued at your writing group, find a developmental editor. This type of editor works with the author on the entire project and performs an in-depth review of its content. The editor will look at the book's structure. My editor helps me with transitions at the beginning and ending of chapters, and makes my prose not sound like a medical professional from my former nursing days. A developmental editor can improve:

- accuracy
- character development
- clarity and continuity
- conciseness
- content
- flow and pacing plot
- point of view
- punctuation, spelling, and grammar
- structure development
- tense, tone, and voice
- transitions and word choice

The editorial process helps the author make the writing coherent and fluid. Both self-published and traditionally published authors need an editor, especially at the beginning of their career. Skipping this step may lead to publishers rejecting your book due to poor quality, and unedited books give self-publishing a bad reputation.

There are many places to find a developmental editor. I asked Eva Marie Everson, the director of the Florida Christian Writers Conference and cofounder of Word Weavers International. She has an editing company called Pen in Hand. Christian Editor Connection (CEC) personally matches authors with established Christian editors who have been extensively screened. These professionals offer developmental editing, copyediting, proofreading, ghostwriting, mentoring, and more. Each CEC editor must have at least two years of paid editing experience, provide references, and pass rigorous tests for each type of editing they offer. This matchmaking service is free to authors. To find an editor who is just right for you and your project, go to ChristianEditor.com and click to Request an Editor. See appendix 2 for a list of editorial resources.

Send the first chapter of your book to a few editors to edit and provide an estimate for editing your entire manuscript. Some editors charge by the hour, while others charge by the page. You want to find an editor that you feel comfortable with and edits your work well. Without my editor, Janis Whipple, I would not have multiple award-winning books. She turns my scientific prose into language everyone can understand. An award-winning book sells better and gives you a marketing edge.

A professional editor can elevate and enhance your writing, which will give you the best chance of successfully communicating your message to readers. A well-polished book can escalate your marketing efforts, resulting in an exponential increase in sales.

Ask for Reviews at the End of Your Book

Readers enjoy engaging with authors. Put your contact information such as website, email, or both in either a brief paragraph or letter to the reader from you—the author—at the end of your book. If a reader contacts you, thank them for communicating with you and ask them to post a book review. Explain how their review will help other potential readers discover the benefits of the book as they have.

Summary

Ecclesiastes 4:12 says, "Though one may be overpowered, two can defend themselves. A cord of three strands is not quickly broken" (NIV). Picture your writing as a tapestry, woven with the golden threads of your prose, interlaced with the strength of a Christian writers' group, and fortified by the discerning eye of a skilled editor. Together they form a threefold cord—not quickly broken—that elevates your work beyond the ordinary.

For authors, the pursuit of refining their writing craft—grammar skills, word choice, structure, outlines, and advanced writing techniques—represents an ongoing journey of artistic growth. You can compare this process to navigating an intricate trail system. Just as hikers rely on posted signage to traverse paths safely and efficiently, writers must understand the rules and guardrails that comprise the author's craft. This hard-earned comprehension acts as a compass, guiding your pen (and fingers on the keyboard) to ensure your narratives flow with clarity and purpose. An outline can save time and improve the overall quality of a book. Proper usage of language reveals the purest expression of your inner passion for the message God planted within you. With patience, dedication, and perpetual learning, writers equip themselves to navigate the challenging terrain of storytelling.

When you embrace these strategies, you'll find that publishers take notice, drawn by the quality and depth of your craftsmanship. Your readers will find a profound joy in the pages you pen.

Action Steps

1. Determine if your writing style is a plotter or a pantser.
2. Figure out the best time of day for you to write, and schedule writing into your calendar.
3. Create your book's outline.
4. Write without editing.
5. Join a Christian writers' group in your area or online.

6. Read writing-craft books to improve your prose.
7. Use a paid version of an online editor to edit your work.
8. Decide whether to use beta readers, and if so, identify them.
9. Edit your manuscript.
10. Find a developmental editor to edit your manuscript.

Chapter 2

Define Your Ministry and Audience

As a Christian author, recognizing your calling is foundational before advancing in your writing career. Similar to a pastor called to preach, you are called to write with a purpose that transcends personal gain—your writing is a ministry intended to further the kingdom of God. Embrace this holy vocation with dedication and seek guidance from God in this divinely appointed journey.

The path of a Christian writer often involves exploring uncharted territories, marked by uncertainties about which writing genre or specific ministry to pursue. It's normal to experience a sense of uncertainty as you carve out your niche in the literary world. The process of discovering the right genre for your message requires you to explore a deeper understanding of your personal interests and what the market demands. This journey may involve trial and error as you move out of your comfort zone to determine what God has designed you to create.

I know it did for me. After writing my first book, *Scripture Yoga*, I thought I was limited to writing only about types of exercise, but I soon realized that wasn't true. Members of my Word Weaver writers' group encouraged me to expand my horizons, pointing out that my expertise could cover a broader range of topics within the healthy living field. Their advice opened new doors for me, and I embraced the opportunity to write on a wider array of subjects.

Some opportunities may not pan out, but these experiences often lead to new paths that feel as though they were meant to be. For example, after most of my devotional submissions were rejected, I realized my strength did not lie in writing devotionals but in creating nonfiction works that blend scientific insight with elements of Christianity. This realization helped me discern my divine writing path, which feels like it was meant for me all along. With each turn in your path, seek God's help with defining your writing ministry.

Define Your Ministry Vision and Mission

Before stepping further into this career, you must identify your ministry, brand, and audience. In defining your ministry, establish a clear vision and mission for your writing. Of course, you must begin with a sense of God's call into this venture and the faith that he has designed you for this path. Then identify your vision, which is a measurable description of where you want your business to go or the impact you desire to make on the world. The vision should articulate a concrete, achievable future for your ministry. My vision was to positively affect the Centers for Disease Control statistic that 42 percent of Americans suffered from obesity. I wanted to decrease that statistic through my healthy living books.

Next, create a mission statement for your company that clearly defines the purpose of your ministry—why it exists and its value to your vision and those you desire to influence. Your mission statement should be clear, concise, and easy to understand. For example, as a writer, my mission statement is to inspire others to improve their health so they can serve God better.

For my author association business, the Christian Indie Publishing Association's (CIPA) vision statement is "To become the premier Christian small publishing and indie author association. To be recognized for its value, discounts, and training." And CIPA's mission statement is to "Equip Christian small publishers and indie authors with tools, resources, and discounts to sell more books. To help authors get their God-given message into the hands of more readers."

Manage your ministry as a business. Set up a separate checking account and credit card to better manage finances and track the fiscal health of your publishing efforts. In chapter 6, Navigate the Publishing Journey: Traditional versus Self-Publishing, we will discuss whether you should set up a publishing imprint for your business.

As a business owner, you'll need to decide between establishing a limited liability corporation (LLC) or operating as a sole proprietorship. An LLC offers the advantage of protecting personal assets from business debts and liabilities; whereas sole proprietors are personally liable for business debts and obligations, which can pose a risk to personal assets. For those concerned about liability, forming an LLC is the wiser choice.

I established a limited liability corporation for my business—Christian Indie Publishing, LLC. Creating an LLC can be a strategic move if you're looking to elevate your business's credibility. Each state has its own regulations and procedures for setting up an LLC. In Florida, for example, the process involved filling out an online application and making a payment to the state, after which I received my Employer Identification Number (EIN). An EIN, also known as a federal tax identification number, is used to identify a business entity. However, if you operate as a sole proprietor without employees, forming a limited liability corporation might not be necessary.

Create a Business Plan with Goals and Strategies

As a Christian author embarking on a new career, it's important to first clarify your mission and goals. What has God called you to write about? How does your writing serve his kingdom? Pray and reflect on these questions to define your purpose in writing. As you begin to work on a new project, make sure it fits into your overall purpose. You may be excited about a new idea, but make sure it supports the mission and vision you have established. An idea that doesn't may find its place later, however, so don't discard it completely. As you execute your vision, set specific, measurable goals to track your progress. For example, you might aim to finish your next manuscript by a certain date.

With your goals in mind, develop strategies that will help you achieve them. Consider the different avenues you could take to spread your message effectively. This might include writing a series of blog posts, launching a podcast tour, or conducting speaking engagements. For each strategy, outline the steps needed to execute it and set deadlines to ensure its progress.

Given such a wide range of possible activities, learn to prioritize tasks that align closely with your goals. What project should you accomplish first? Identify the most impactful strategies for that specific endeavor and focus your energy there. Goals should be measurable and defined by a length of time, such as completing the first draft of your next book within six months or growing your social media following by 20 percent before your next book launch.

For example, these were my top five goals this year:

1. Every month write three thousand words of my book *How to Sell 1,000 Books a Month*.
2. Launch my new book, *12 Ways to Age Gracefully*. Follow my marketing plan. Solicit podcasts to ensure I have an interview monthly.
3. Continue to manage Christian Authors Network and Christian Indie Publishing Association.
4. Improve my 7 *Steps* email sequence; add affiliate links to high-priced items. (You'll find more information on what this means in chapter 3.)
5. Need to relax more both physically and mentally.

Next, detail the specific actions required to move your strategies forward. This may involve learning about some industries you don't yet know much about. Marketing activities are multifaceted, so educate yourself on areas with which you are unfamiliar. For instance, if your approach includes a podcast tour, you might start by researching podcasts about your area of content, and then contacting hosts for opportunities. Each action should be a step toward achieving one of your priorities, clearly contributing to your overall mission.

Consolidate your business's vision, mission, strategic plans, goals, and actions into a clear, concise one-to-two-page document. This plan will serve as your roadmap, keeping you focused and motivated. Regularly review and adjust your plan as needed to stay on track with your career objectives. Sharing this plan with a mentor or fellow Christian authors can provide valuable feedback and accountability.

Your business plan is not just a formal document; it's a dynamic tool that guides your career as a Christian author. As you set clear goals, develop strategic plans, prioritize tasks, and take decisive actions, you can ensure that your writing journey is not only faithful to your calling but also effective in reaching the hearts and minds of your readers.

At the end of the year, review the plan and celebrate the progress your ministry attained. Evaluate your plan to ensure your business is moving in the right direction. Adjust your business plan as needed.

Perseverance plays a critical role in your success. Maintain your resilience through the highs and lows, learn from each experience, and continually refine your skills to fulfill the ministry God has set before you.

Perform Annual Planning

At the beginning of each year, reevaluate your business's vision, mission, goals, and strategic plan. I typically conduct this planning session during the week after Christmas when business activities slow down.

To create and evaluate an annual plan as a Christian author, start by seeking divine guidance. Begin your planning session with prayer, asking God to direct you through the year ahead. Spend time in meditation, allowing God's voice to influence your goals and decisions. Choose a scripture verse to serve as your guiding theme for the new year, to help focus your actions and decisions in alignment with biblical principles. This year I chose Deuteronomy 15:10 "Give generously to them and do so without a grudging heart; then because of this the LORD your God will bless you in all your work and in everything you put your hand to" (NIV).

Reflect on your achievements from the previous year, especially as they relate to your business plan. Celebrate your success, as this recognition provides a sense of accomplishment and helps you see the tangible results of your efforts. Don't despair over goals not met. Instead, evaluate what was successful and what wasn't. Determine which parts of your life or business you should change or eliminate to pursue your calling and goals. This might include letting go of unproductive habits or reconsidering commitments that don't align with your vision.

Set specific, measurable goals for the coming year to accomplish your business plan. Organize these goals by their priority and establish a timeline for achieving them, breaking them down into monthly or quarterly segments. To stay on track, regularly review and adjust your annual plan each quarter. This continual assessment allows for flexibility and responsiveness to the changing dynamics of your life and career as a Christian author. Regularly revisit your goals to ensure your actions remain aligned with both your professional ambitions and your spiritual growth.

Consider outsourcing certain tasks by hiring staff when appropriate, particularly in areas that are not your strong suit. Decide which areas you can learn or already understand and which areas you should outsource for reasons of time or skill. For instance, it's more efficient for me to pay an hourly rate for a virtual assistant to handle technical aspects of my business than to spend an entire day struggling with them myself, only to potentially fail. Such setbacks can really drain my motivation and energy. Check out AlyssaAvantAndCompany.com who specializes in virtual assistant and administrative support for Christian authors.

Therefore, I employ a virtual assistant, graphic designer, and webmaster on an as-needed basis. They are not my employees but independent contractors. While their services are not constantly required in my writing business, the time and frustration they save me are invaluable. To find further information about annual planning, see appendix 1.

Identify Your Values

Once you have your ministry and plan defined, the next step on your path is to determine your values to ensure you attract readers whose beliefs align with yours. When your messaging truly reflects your core values, it naturally attracts followers who share those beliefs. When your branding and communications consistently embody these values, you create a strong resonance with your audience.

Values represent the intrinsic beliefs shaping your behaviors, perspectives, and approach to life. While attitudes may ebb and flow, core values remain your unwavering guiding principles. Examine the following list of potential core values:

- abundance
- acceptance
- accountability
- accuracy
- achievement
- adventure
- advocacy

- ambition
- appreciation
- attractiveness
- authenticity
- authority
- autonomy
- balance
- beauty
- benevolence
- boldness
- bliss
- bravery
- brilliance
- calmness
- caring
- challenges
- charity
- cheerfulness
- Christianity
- citizenship
- clarity
- cleanliness
- cleverness
- community
- compassion
- competency
- contribution
- cooperation
- collaboration
- consistency
- contribution
- courage
- creativity
- credibility

- curiosity
- daring
- decisiveness
- dependability
- dependency
- determination
- diversity
- efficiency
- encouragement
- enthusiasm
- ethics
- excellence
- expressiveness
- fairness
- faith
- family
- flexibility
- forgiveness
- freedom
- friendships
- fun
- generosity
- goodness
- grace
- gratitude
- growth
- happiness
- harmony
- health
- honesty
- honor
- hope
- humility
- humor

- independence
- individuality
- influence
- innovation
- insightfulness
- inspiration
- integrity
- intelligence
- intuition
- joy
- justice
- kindness
- knowledge
- leadership
- learning
- love
- loyalty
- making a difference
- meaningful work
- mercy
- mindfulness
- motivation
- openness
- optimism
- originality
- passion
- patience
- performance
- personal development
- peace
- perfection
- playfulness
- pleasure
- popularity

Define Your Ministry and Audience

- power
- preparedness
- proactivity
- professionalism
- prosperity
- punctuality
- quality
- recognition
- relationships
- reliability
- religion
- reputation
- resilience
- respect
- resourcefulness
- responsibility
- responsiveness
- risk taking
- security
- self-control
- selflessness
- self-love
- self-respect
- service
- simplicity
- sincerity
- spirituality
- stability
- status
- success
- teamwork
- thankfulness
- thoughtfulness
- traditionalism

- trustworthiness
- understanding
- uniqueness
- usefulness
- versatility
- vision
- wealth
- well-being
- wisdom
- zeal

Carefully identify which values on this list resonate within you and circle them. Then group the circled values into three-to-five overarching themes. Condense each group down to a single word or short phrase capturing its essence. These theme descriptors illuminate the key values you should infuse into all your branding.

Your communication should incorporate those values that resonate with your readers who share similar beliefs. Include these values in your lead magnets, email journey, blog entries, products, and overall brand communication.

Find Your Audience

After you've identified your ministry, vision, and writing genre, determine your target audience. And this audience should be large and specific. Are they Christians or not?

Many new writers think their audience is everyone. When an author attempts to write to everyone, they actually write to no one. It is imperative to determine your target readership. Neglecting this essential step ensures your book will struggle to find its market. When you clearly define your target reader, you can effectively connect with them. If you don't, few will buy your book. You need to market it to your precise readership for maximum discoverability and appeal.

For my first book, *Scripture Yoga*, my target audience was Christians who perform yoga. This was a specific target market, but it was not large. Therefore, I did not attain high book sales. So I expanded my audience with my second book, *Yoga for Beginners*, to people who want to learn how to perform yoga. And the book was secular, so the readers did not have be Christians. This readership was larger than my first book, and I sold more copies.

With my third book, *7 Steps to Get Off Sugar and Carbohydrates*, I derived my audience from this Centers for Disease Control statistic: half of Americans live with a chronic illness and 42 percent are obese. Finally my target audience was large enough to merit high book sales.

If your target audience is not specific and not large, you will not sell a thousand books a month. My first two books never did. So of all the ideas you have for books, choose one that would have a large, specific readership. This is key to attaining high book sales.

Besides understanding your own values, to form a connection with your followers, you must intimately understand your audience's deepest pains, failed solutions, and unmet needs:

- What is their biggest, most persistent struggle?
- Why does this challenge cause them such torment?
- If you could magically solve their problem, what would that solution look like?
- What past efforts or products did they try that left them unfulfilled?
- What rare instances brought them fleeting relief?
- How do they like to destress?
- How can your story take them away?
- What does your common value system offer them to meet their needs?
- How does your message intersect their pain?

By understanding the experience of your audience, you can

vividly explore how your personal journey, teachings, and offerings can act as the support they've been desperately seeking.

Next, your reader must benefit from your prose. Does your fiction book transport them away to a foreign land with adventure? Does your nonfiction work help them recover from an addiction? Whether self-help or entertainment, your book must reward the reader. It must be worth their money to buy it and time to read it.

Everyone enjoys a story. Even nonfiction authors weave stories into their prose to engage the reader. Jesus used parables. In my self-help book, I combined practical insights with a personal account of how I guided my sister to stop eating sugar and carbs, which helped her lose weight and cure a chronic ailment.

Instead of writing a memoir, choose to write a personal growth book that will help the reader learn from your life's journey. Weave parts of your story, and the stories of others as well, into the chapters as examples. Most readers do not want to read about someone's life unless they are famous. But they may choose to learn from you in a nonfiction Christian living book.

You could turn your memoir into a novel that may interest readers. I met an author at a conference who was writing a fiction book that included the dysfunctional relationships she had endured in her life. Her heroine grew and learned to recognize inappropriate patterns and how to change.

Many of us write from our own tragedies. Romans 8:28 states, "And we know that God causes everything to work together for the good of those who love God and are called according to his purpose for them" (NLT). We want to help others who have also suffered. Our writing is a way for us to affect many more lives positively—even after we die.

Does your book idea meet a need in the market? Research current trends in the publishing world through searching on Christian Book Distributor (ChristianBook.com) for Christian books and Amazon for secular books. Look for books similar to yours to determine how saturated the market is on that subject. During the pandemic, children's nonfiction science, technology, education, and math (STEM) books were trending. Writing to the market's demand could land you with excellent book sales. Or find a gap in the market. For a while, there were not many boy-oriented middle-grade novels.

Incorporate emotions and experiences in your book. Write from your own meaningful life situations such as abuse, abandonment, or infertility. Do you have a story inside of you that you could put on paper as if the reader were experiencing it themselves? Your villain could portray someone from your past. Emotion and vulnerability catch the reader in your grasp. Our stories are powerful.

Whatever you decide to write, hook the reader on the back cover and in the first paragraph of your book. A potential reader may check these areas first before deciding to purchase your book. What is in it for the reader—describe that in the first paragraph of a nonfiction book. For fiction, start with the most amazing action scene. You only have a few seconds of your potential readers' attention before they choose to buy your book. Snag them.

My hook for *7 Steps to Get Off Sugar and Carbohydrates* was "Would you like to improve the way you feel and look while increasing your energy level and clarity of mind? How about losing weight naturally without going on a fad diet or buying prepared meals and supplements? You can achieve these results by simply changing the food you eat." Apparently, this hook is working because I sell loads of books.

The book cover must draw in the reader and fit with the genre of your book. Check the thumbnail version (the small image viewers see when scrolling through an online list of books) of your cover to ensure you can clearly read the title and see any image. Can you tell from the title what fiction genre the book is in or what the nonfiction book is about? The book's title should portray its topic and include keywords so your target audience can easily find it.

Build Your Brand

Once you have defined your values, ministry, and audience, the next essential task is to develop a strong personal brand. Branding is more than just a logo or color scheme. It's about creating a cohesive image that communicates your values and resonates with your audience.

Start by hiring a professional photographer for a high-quality headshot. This photo should reflect the professional image you want to convey and be suitable for use across all your platforms. Update your headshot about every five years.

Dressing in colors that complement your skin tone and hair color will significantly enhance your appearance in professional photos. I had a personal color analysis performed and found it to be an invaluable tool. This analysis provided me with a flattering color palette that helps me understand which clothing, makeup, and jewelry colors look best on me.

The next step is to establish your brand colors. Working with a professional graphic designer or a branding coach can help you choose colors and fonts that appeal to you and your audience and reflect the tone of your ministry. Fonts convey subtle messages about a company. A traditional font projects respectability that financial or publishing companies want to portray. Whereas an elegant font may appear more with luxury and artistic brands. Once you select your colors and fonts, create a branding sheet that includes your choices to use in all your marketing materials.

A branding sheet ensures uniformity across your website, social media profiles, and printed materials. All the personnel you work with should have a copy of your sheet. Branding extends to every aspect of your online and offline presence. Ensure that all printed and online marketing materials reflect the same color schemes, font styles, and overall aesthetic. This consistency helps reinforce your brand identity and makes your materials instantly recognizable to your audience. For example, use the same headshot and banner across all your social media profiles.

For your book, consider creating a professional one-sheet that includes key information about the book, your bio, and a compelling description—all styled in your brand's design. Give the one-sheet to retailers, media, and readers so they will know more about you and your book. Additionally, have your cover designer create 3D shots of your book cover to add a polished look to your promotional materials, making your book more attractive to potential readers and buyers.

Effective branding is crucial for authors because it not only helps establish a connection with the audience but also sets the professional tone of their career. A well-crafted brand can significantly affect your visibility and success in the competitive book publishing market.

Foster Connections with Exclusive Facebook Groups

Would you like to develop deeper connections with your readers? Closed Facebook groups offer a unique platform for doing just that. Many writers opt for public author pages, but in a closed group, only members can view and engage with content, creating a more intimate setting. The environment you create in your group should focus on how you, as the author, can enrich the lives of the members. Picture hosting a Bible study in your home. You are the leader who offers valuable insights and fosters relationships among group attendees. Similarly, Facebook groups enhance engagement and offer mutual benefits for the author and members.

Your primary goal should be to offer members content that either entertains or helps them. In my exclusive Facebook group How to Sell 1,000 Books a Month, I share leads for bloggers, podcasters, and show hosts looking for interviews, along with crucial marketing advice. I'm not just there to answer questions; I encourage members to push their limits, offering feedback on their marketing plans to help them grow. This group complements my course How to Sell 1,000 Books in 3 Months at CIPA.Podia.com.

My second group caters to those seeking advice on healthy living. Members ask many questions regarding health, nutrition, and how to change their eating habits. I thoroughly enjoy engaging with my audience and providing them with the support they need to make difficult lifestyle changes. The interaction and support within this group has been remarkable, with members stepping in to assist and encourage one another, creating a network of heartfelt connections. Anyone seeking to make positive lifestyle changes is welcome to join this group—7 Steps to Get Off Sugar, Carbs, and Gluten on Facebook at Facebook.com/groups/184355458927013. Opening your group to all, regardless of whether they've purchased your book or course, can lead to sales down the line if they find value in the community.

For authors, these groups are invaluable as you expand your reach and build a personal connection with your audience. These spaces allow you to build trust and loyalty as you engage directly with your followers, answer their questions, and provide them with valuable information. A group can also serve as a bridge to increase your email list. In the request to enter the Facebook group, you can ask up to three initial questions to potential members. One key question I include asks for their email address to subscribe to my newsletter. While I did not make it a mandatory field for group entry, the majority willingly share their emails. This increases my ability to market future offerings to those who would benefit.

Managing the influx of new members, especially given the thousands that have joined, required a significant amount of my time. Therefore, I use an external service, Group Collector at groupcollector.com, to streamline the process. This tool not only approves new members automatically but also organizes their information on a Google sheet and integrates their email addresses directly into my mailing service. To gain more members in this group, I've incorporated an invitation to this exclusive Facebook group within several of my self-published books. When you have a new book or product, you can easily let your followers know about it through your Facebook group and your expanded email list.

To make your Facebook group discoverable, link it across your digital presence—your website, Amazon author page, the bio sections of your articles and blogs, and your Facebook author page. An exclusive Facebook group gives readers direct access to you, enabling a deeper connection and understanding of how you can add value to their lives. Ultimately, exclusive Facebook groups are a beneficial platform for fostering meaningful interactions and community among readers and authors alike.

Summary

As you embark on your path as a Christian author, establishing a clear understanding of your ministry and audience lays a crucial foundation for your career. By creating a vision and mission, you align your writing career with your spiritual calling. Your creative works will inspire and serve a higher purpose.

This chapter has guided you through identifying your calling, understanding your audience, and aligning your professional goals with your spiritual aspirations. Keep these principles in mind as you navigate the complexities of the literary world, trusting in God's guidance, and embracing each challenge as an opportunity for growth. As you progress, continue to reflect on and refine your approach, ensuring each step you take not only furthers your career but also contributes to the expansion of God's kingdom through your words.

Action Steps

1. Pray and reflect on the divine purpose behind your writing to identify your divine calling.
2. Establish a clear vision statement for your writing career.
3. Write a mission statement explaining the purpose of your writing ministry.
4. Create a document outlining your business's vision, mission, goals, and strategies.

5. Perform annual planning and schedule quarterly reviews of your plan.
6. Consider hiring support, such as a virtual assistant, graphic designer, or webmaster, to handle aspects of your business that are outside of your expertise.
7. Identify your intrinsic values and ensure your brand and promotional materials reflect your values.
8. Determine your target audience and how you can help them through your writing ministry.
9. Get a professional headshot to use with your branding.
10. Develop your brand, including a branding sheet.

Chapter 3

Build an Author Platform

You've worked on a manuscript and created a message to reach the needs of a particular group of readers. You've improved the writing through a Christian writers' group and a professional editor. So how do you now get that message out to the right audience?

It's time to establish your platform. What's that? Just as a speaker reaches an audience from an actual platform, authors need a vehicle from which to launch their message. So in publishing, a platform refers to an author's overall online presence and ability to connect with potential readers and market their book.

Your words hold immense power to entertain, inspire, and transform lives. Even the most heartfelt messages need a stage to effectively reach those who need to hear them. This chapter will teach you the steps to meet that goal.

As you publicize your message, don't become overwhelmed by the multitude of platform-building tasks. Constructing a platform is a dynamic process that requires patience and dedication. You can't complete all these tasks at once. Break up the assignments into phases by drafting a strategic roadmap that charts reasonable milestones to accomplish. As you meet each goal, you increase the potential to reach more readers. Writing is a journey; with each step, you will amplify your message.

Design Your Website

In today's digital world, an impactful website is essential for establishing your author brand and connecting with readers. If you don't already have one, creating a professional website should be a top priority. Your site will serve as the central hub where your audience discovers you, learns more about your work, engages with your content, and even purchases your book.

First, you need to purchase a domain name. This is essentially your website name, or the text a user types into a web browser to reach a particular site. The ideal option is to use your author name. It is the simplest way to promote your overall vision and mission. However, if another user has already registered your name, get creative by incorporating your middle initial or exploring other alternatives. The key is choosing something clear, memorable, and aligned with your brand.

I could not get SusanNeal.com because a realtor owned it, and she was not willing to sell it to me. So I had to choose from SusanNealAuthor.com, SusanNealRN.com, or SusanUNeal.com. I chose SusanUNeal.com, which included my middle initial. Thereafter, I used my middle initial in my author name on all my books. Now, however, I wish I had chosen SusanNealRN.com. At that time, I did not realize all my books would be in the healthy living genre and the registered nurse (RN) designation would have lent credentials to that field.

If you write across multiple genres or own a separate business, using your author name as a website remains the best approach. Many authors effectively use their website's Home page as a navigational portal for visitors. There visitors can choose different sections tailored to each interest, or go to each book, with one simple click.

I've seen websites where the Home page offers both a membership and an author website. The two choices lead to two different website areas.

Avoid using book titles for your website name, as that option becomes quickly outdated with subsequent book releases. Instead, purchase your desired name as the primary domain name. You can optionally acquire additional domains that connect back to your website from a reliable domain registrar. Owning additional website names allows you to cover extra access points that readers may use to find you online. For example, ScriptureYoga.com and ChristianYoga.com go to my same website. I simply had my webmaster direct the domain name ScriptureYoga.com to the site. Search various domain registrar sites to purchase yours.

Craft an Engaging Online Presence

Building a website requires a lot of steps to create an effective home for your online presence. You want to be sure your site offers visual appeal, appropriate and updated information on your message, and an interesting reason for potential readers to return. Most importantly, it must represent you and your brand.

Even though some authors could create at least a basic website, I recommend hiring a professional. Even if you hire an expert to construct your site, you still need to make decisions about its design and content. Make sure you have input and approval in the process. After all, it's your name on the site. My webmaster gave me a link to look at every WordPress website template so I could choose what resonated with my style and brand.

First impressions matter, so crafting a visually appealing look and feel is your first priority. Use the branding sheet we discussed in chapter 2, which includes your brand colors and fonts. Being consistent with your branding is fundamental to ensure your audience easily recognizes you.

Consider investing in professional photography that aligns with your brand identity and writing, and not just for your headshots but for photos on your website to illustrate your values and personality. A photo shoot in your home, garden, or other settings relevant to your work can provide authentic visuals that welcome readers into your world.

I hired a photographer friend to do a photo shoot at my home. Inside my kitchen we took photos of me chopping colorful vegetables and arranging flowers. In the living room, I posed reading a Bible by my fireplace. My ninth book, *12 Ways to Age Gracefully*, featured one of those photos on its cover with my mother-in-law and me picking fruit in my orchard. She was eighty-seven, and I was fifty-seven in the photo.

If hiring a photographer isn't feasible, explore high-quality stock image libraries like pixabay.com, unsplash.com, and canva.com. Ensure these sites provide you with the legal rights to use the images. Don't borrow images from someone else's site or other online spots without implicit permission to use them. However, photos featuring you personally can forge a deeper connection with audiences interested in the person behind the pages. Be sure you give photo credit on your website for your stock images, if you use them, and credit to a professional if you choose one.

Next, map the website's architecture. Decide which pages to include and what content belongs on each page. Research several authors' websites in your genre to spark ideas, but don't mimic their pages. Reflect on how to capture your brand creatively to resonate with your target readers. Even if you've hired a professional to build your site, you need to be engaged in the research and content preparation. The more you know your site, the better you'll be able to manage it once it's built.

Once you've outlined potential pages, solicit feedback from writing peers, friends, and your writing group. Remember the cord of three strands? I always ask others to help me brainstorm my book titles, website content, and topics to include in my book. Collaboration breeds innovation, so embrace diverse perspectives in this foundational design phase of your website. Some of these same people may also help you launch your book when it's ready. (See chapter 7 on the book launch.) They'll already be familiar with your brand, mission, and message from your website.

Incorporate these top five essential pages into your site: Home, About, Contact, Shop, and Blog. The Home page is your make-or-break opener, so invest time in adding persuasive hooks that entice visitors to keep exploring your content. Grab the reader with benefits for them. Portray how you can transform their lives for the better, or whisk them away on a fantasy journey, or help them lose weight. I learned to create a viewer-focused website from *Sell Your Book Like Wildfire* by Rob Eager.

Prioritize your email list growth by prominently featuring an opt-in opportunity for a valuable lead magnet (a free gift in exchange for their email address) at the top of your website Home page. Supplement this with a well-timed pop-up nudging visitors to subscribe. Create your opt-in gift beforehand so it is ready for your website launch. An exciting opt-in and an engaged email audience is invaluable for any author's long-term success. (We will discuss free gifts and email sequences later in this chapter.)

While the Home page aims to captivate visitors, the About section allows you to foster deeper connections by positioning yourself as their guide in this area of life. Tell the viewer more about you but from the perspective of how you can entertain them or solve their problem. How do your credentials, experience, or imagination uniquely equip you to solve your readers' challenges? Convey the empathy and authenticity that reassures them you genuinely understand their needs.

The Contact page serves as the gateway for audiences to initiate personal exchanges with you. Provide your email address as the primary channel for inquiries. You may wish to establish an email address just for your author life and leave your private email for the rest. Some authors also list phone numbers, though most opt for email only to maintain boundaries.

For privacy, avoid publishing your home address. You might also offer an integrated calendar to streamline scheduling interviews or events. Remember, your website is not just for potential book readers but for those who will help you market it. You'll be giving out your online information through your one-sheet. You never know who may visit, so make sure you are providing all anyone may need to know.

An e-commerce enabled shop is a must for selling books, courses, and other products or services tied to your brand. This shop extends your ability to sell products to your audience beyond the book format. For example, you could sell supplementary portable document format (PDF) packets, video or audio courses, and other premium content that expands upon your literary work at higher profit margins compared to book sales. These other products will in turn help you sell more books as you cross-promote.

I've got DVDs, CDs, ebooks, and digital products for sale on my shop at susanuneal.com/shop. You can make more money selling a PDF than you can a book. For example, I created and sell the pamphlet How to Prevent, Improve, and Reverse Alzheimer's and Dementia on my website for $5. However, I receive about $3 profit per book sale.

It is difficult to support your ministry through book sales alone. You need to create other revenue sources. My course 7 Steps to Reclaim Your Health and Optimal Weight at SusanUNeal.com sells for $97. I also became a certified author coach, so I provide coaching to writers as well. Revenue from coaching and courses helps pay my writing ministry bills. You will learn more about financially supporting yourself in chapter 11.

Make it easy for website visitors to connect with you across other online channels by prominently displaying your social media icons. If you are not currently active on the primary social media platforms—Facebook, Instagram, LinkedIn, Pinterest—be sure you've set up accounts in all of them and engage with them often. Incorporate these linked icons into website footers, sidebars, your Contact page, or a combination of highly visible areas. You want your audience to follow your activities with a simple click through your social media posts. Unfortunately, I find many author websites do not include their social media icons.

Are you going to blog? Consistent blogging is time consuming, but it offers powerful rewards for improving your website's search engine ranking. Each new blog post acts as fresh content that appeals to search engine algorithms, which frequently search for relevant material on the web. If you use strategic keywords and other search engine optimization (SEO) techniques in your blogs, you can elevate your site's visibility on search engines like Google. To learn more about this topic read the section Driving Website Traffic: The Power of Strategic Blogging, in chapter 5.

No matter which path you choose, ensure your website provides a user-friendly experience that immerses visitors into the key messages and benefits of your brand. An enticing website lays the crucial groundwork for forging enduring connections with your readership. The Home page hooks them, the About section humanizes the experience, the Contact page facilitates dialogue, and your Shop empowers you to monetize your expertise. A robust website is the starting point of your platform.

Build Your Email Subscribers

While blogging forges connections through its content, a well-architected email marketing sequence gives your readers a personalized peek into your world. Before diving into your email series, you must understand your core values as an author and have a well-defined brand as we discussed in chapter 2. Your intrinsic beliefs should shape your perspectives and approach. Make your core values your unwavering guiding principles—just like God should be.

Infuse your key values into your lead magnets and email journey. Aligning your messaging with your authentic values attracts kindred spirits—subscribers whose belief systems match yours. This values-based resemblance cultivates powerful rapport and trust with your email subscribers. All your communication should resonate, "You get me" to your readers.

To form a connection with their values, you must intimately understand your audience's deepest pains, failed solutions, and unmet needs, as reviewed in chapter 2. Understanding your audience enables you to focus on how your personal journey and teachings shared in your emails can provide the support your subscribers seek.

Speak to Your Readers' Intimate Struggles

Once you've established the values you want to communicate and the needs of your email readers that you can help with your message, craft the content to reach them. You'll want to establish a series of emails that will build and reinforce your messages. With the groundwork of your values to draw readers in, you can purposefully create an email experience that resonates holistically with them to keep readers opening future correspondence from you. Determine how you'll entice new subscribers to opt-in to your email list, and what specific journey you'll escort them through in your narratives.

- How can your stories and perspective cultivate an intimate rapport?
- What uplifting lessons will you share to light their path forward?
- How can your messaging empower them to embrace change?
- How can you connect with them in their daily lives?

Envision this nurturing email sequence as an engaging fireside chat where you openly share your experiences and wisdom in a relatable, reassuring manner—just like you would with a friend over a cup of coffee. By fusing your authenticity with their deeply felt needs, you transform from a bombardment of impersonal emails into a trusted guide.

Engage Subscribers with Your Lead Magnet

A lead magnet is an enticing gift you offer your audience in exchange for their email information. The opt-in gift must promise premium value. Craft a lead magnet that aligns with your values and brand so you will attract the right audience. The subscriber who signs up should inherently identify with your brand through your magnet. Your gift should foster a sense of shared values that compels them to remain engaged with your subsequent emails.

When planning your magnet, first review the problems and questions your audience needs you to solve. Ensure your giveaway provides a remedy for at least one of their pressing concerns. Many fiction authors offer the first book in a series as their opt-in gift. If they get readers hooked on the first one, they are more likely to purchase subsequent novels in the series.

As a nonfiction author, don't tackle too many of the readers' struggles in your gift. Instead focus on providing an actionable first step for one of their challenges. You want this gift to be the beginning of an ongoing relationship, where they can trust you to provide what they need. You also want this gift to offer enough benefit for them to entrust you with their email address, so you can continue to build on your message.

Guide them gradually by first articulating the "what" and "why," such as what results others achieved through your approach, and why your philosophy beats the alternatives they've tried unsuccessfully. Or express how your words can entertain or enlighten your audience. Give them a checklist or a guide and slowly, through the email automation sequence or newsletter, lead them to your book, course, or coaching program. When your free offering captures their attention, they will be ready to embark on the journey you have planned for them.

While your magnet concepts will undoubtedly evolve over time through evaluation and refinement, the initial offer should directly correlate with what you sell. For example, I publish healthy living books, so my lead magnets Reboot Your Metabolism and Gluten Intolerance Quiz work well. The Home page of my website (SusanUNeal.com) hosts several of my free gifts. I don't sell meal plans, so having a meal plan opt-in gift wouldn't work. Stay in your lane and don't promise what you can't or don't deliver.

Besides nailing your magnet's content and messaging, the following tips will increase your number of subscribers. Buy a separate domain name to use as a link for your opt-in gift. Again, have your webmaster link these back to your main website. For example, I have CandiQuiz.com and GlutenIntoleranceQuiz.com. It is easier to remember CandiQuiz.com rather than SusanUNeal.com/CandiQuiz. These short names provide a natural avenue to tell listeners about them when interviewed on podcasts. Also, create a visually pleasing and persuasive landing page when they click on your link, which sells the benefit of opting in. It is always about what is in it for your viewer. Use your branding colors and make this page appealing.

As you'll likely have multiple audiences, consider crafting targeted lead magnets that align with each group's distinct needs and interests. For example, I have a couple of magnets that cater to my health and wellness readers, while another one speaks directly to writers seeking guidance with creating a media kit. (Learn the ten essential ingredients you should include in your media kit at ChristianPublishers.net/free-gift/.)

Choose an Email Marketing Service

Email marketing service companies provide the infrastructure needed to collect emails into groups and send emails to a list of subscribers. Some good ones to choose from include Constant Contact, Active Campaign, ConvertKit, and MailerLite. Most email providers give a free version for you to use until you get to a high number of contacts. You don't want to pay for an expensive subscription service until you build your list and make money from selling your products.

After you have crafted a persuasive landing page that sells the immense benefit of your giveaway, and you've sent your initial email sequence (see the section below), check your email subscriber rate. A typical rate is 1–2 percent—out of every hundred website visitors, you should obtain one-to-two email subscribers. This may seem modest initially, but it adds up over time, especially if you have several free gifts. If you find low or no conversions, create another opt-in gift. Your lead magnet will progress over time. At first, create something simple like a pamphlet versus a video course, in case viewers are not subscribing. To learn more take my course How to Create a Lead Magnet: Start-to-Finish at CIPA.Podia.com.

Craft an Authentic Email Subscriber Experience

With your opt-in strategy solidified, determine whether to create an automated email sequence or a monthly newsletter. Automations include a prewritten series of emails to each new subscriber over an extended period, like one year. Automated emails should focus on timeless, evergreen content, avoiding seasonal or event-driven subjects. You write the automation email sequence once and then you are done, unless you to choose to revise it after a couple of years.

In contrast, newsletters are created monthly ongoing indefinitely, allowing you to insert more topical messaging. For those preferring a set-it-and-forget-it model (like me), an automation works best.

Once you've completed your automated series of emails, your email service sends it to each new subscriber for the first year (or however long the sequence runs) of their subscription. You schedule the days and times your emails are sent, and the service delivers them.

Regarding the time and day you should send your broadcasts, data shows Tuesdays and Thursdays yield higher open and engagement rates. As for send times, the early morning hours around 8 a.m. Eastern frequently captures maximum attention as subscribers start their days. Data also suggests that you should send an email every seven to ten days.

Thereafter, you can send your subscribers occasional broadcast email updates when you have a new product, offer, or book release. For example, when I am a presenter at a healthy living summit, I send all my health and wellness subscribers the information on how to attend the online event. This is an example of a one-time broadcast email versus an automation.

Send Welcome Emails

No matter the format, captivate new subscribers immediately through an engaging welcome series of two to three emails that emphasize how you can help them. Reveal your origin story, qualifications, and the unique value you provide. Write your emails like an intimate conversation with a friend, offering both authenticity and credibility while laying a foundation of trust.

Consider incorporating a personal video to let your personality and passion shine through unfiltered. Be sure to use quality light and camera and an attractive background to create a personal connection with your readers. I created a nine-minute video explaining how I lost my health with ten medical diagnoses and two surgeries (view video at SusanUNeal.com/LostHealth. I wanted them to know I understood their pain.

Sending a regular email newsletter is a great way to keep in touch with your audience by sharing helpful content. Whether you choose an automated evergreen sequence or a periodically broadcasted newsletter, these communications should enlighten and enrich your subscribers' lives through stories, advice, teachings, and insights closely tied to your message.

Write an Email Sequence

Develop a powerful email sequence that engages and inspires your subscribers. Tell your story to your reader. Share your experience so they know who you are and how you can help them. It's like sitting down and connecting with a friend, which builds a relationship with your subscribers, so they trust you.

Craft an uplifting email sequence where you share relatable struggles, teachable moments of growth, and empowering lessons your readers can apply to their own lives. Each message (around 300 words) should illuminate your hard-earned wisdom while reminding your audience you deeply understand their plights. Your sequence should also be uplifting, leaving your audience with a sense of encouragement despite the struggles you may share. A purposeful email relationship guides people until they are ready to fully embrace your offerings as the help they need.

Ultimately, the core mission behind all your emails should center on fostering connections with your tribe. Frame each communication as if you're having a one-on-one conversation with the reader. Keep your ideal reader in mind when writing. Impart your personal narrative and accumulated wisdom. When you show how you understand their desires and needs and paint yourself as a guide who has faced similar hurdles in your personal journey, you cultivate invaluable trust and loyalty.

If you are not sure what to write, pull topics from your books, your individual circumstances, or the most popular blogs you've written. Check your website statistics to see which blogs have had the most views. To nurture the bonds you are developing with your readers, incorporate interactive elements in the emails—ask them questions, ask for prayer requests, or request creative input from your readers. Some authors solicit their subscribers' input on book titles, book covers, and other significant publishing milestones. These interactive emails could be part of the automated sequence or added as a one-time broadcast email.

Make them feel included and engaged by giving them behind-the-scenes access to your world. This personal touch shows them they are part of your inner circle. As my subscribers email me back, I can simply answer their question or also suggest they take my course or sign up for my coaching. It is difficult to support a ministry from book sales alone. We need to create other pricier products and services and lead our readers to them. These options not only help us financially in our author business and ministry but help our readers with additional resources.

Add Strategic Promotional Offers

As you integrate strategic promotional offers of your products, also include affiliate offers. Affiliate sales involve promoting another business's product or service and earning a commission when your email subscribers make a purchase. Commissions through affiliate sales is another way to generate income, especially if it is for a higher-priced item. But be careful. You don't want your emails to be sales driven. Many experts recommend a 5:1 ratio of value-driven content to intentional sales. Give your subscriber five benefit emails before introducing one of your sales offers.

What would make your newsletter reader walk away feeling as though they received something valuable? What can you give them to generate a good feeling? You want your reader to think, *I love getting those emails.* When you consistently deliver enriching, audience-attuned newsletters, a promotional element feels like a welcome opportunity rather than intrusive and salesy.

In my author friend's email, she asks people for prayer requests and provides a specific phone number for a prayer line. You want subscribers to know you're going out of your way to help them. With time, they will trust you. They want to know about you and your struggles. If they trust and believe in you, they will buy most of your books and products.

For information about crafting your lead magnet, creating your email sequence, or building your author platform, please see appendix 1 for author resources.

Summary

Delivering your message to your specific readers requires intentional effort through your author platform. While there are many ways to market your book, your website is the foundation of your platform. No matter how you design your website, it needs to be easy to use and reflect what your company is about. A captivating website serves as the road for establishing lasting bonds with your audience. It draws them in to find out more about you and how you can help them. A well-crafted website marks the beginning of establishing your platform.

The next step is to set up your lead magnet and email subscriber journey. With these in place, you will not only grow your followers but also deepen your impact in their lives. Your marketing isn't just about building a platform; it's about constructing a digital pulpit.

Action Steps

1. Buy at least one domain name for your website.
2. Schedule a photo shoot in your home, garden, or other setting relevant to your work. Use the photos in your website.
3. Develop a professional author website.
4. Create a lead magnet and its landing page. Monitor how often the lead magnet is being downloaded to gain email subscribers.
5. Buy a memorable domain name for your lead magnet to share during interviews.

6. Select an email marketing service provider to manage your subscriber list.
7. Connect your lead magnet's landing page to your email marketing provider.
8. Write an automated welcome email sequence (two to three emails in one week).
9. Produce either a newsletter or automated email sequence sent every seven to ten days
10. Add affiliate offers to your emails to generate additional income.

Chapter 4

Embark on the Journey of Newfound Knowledge

Now that you've started your writing career, it's time to seek wisdom and understanding about the craft and industry you're stepping into. Writers' conferences are like wellsprings of knowledge, bubbling with insights and connections that can nourish your budding career. Whether you are a new writer just beginning the literary journey or a seasoned author, you will benefit from a writers' conference.

As a newbie, don't be intimidated by the idea of attending, because you will not be alone. And while many conferees may be more experienced in the writing journey, everyone has more to learn. You will also gain knowledge by listening to what others have discovered along the way, and you'll be encouraged by how much support you find. Every writer I have ever met has been happy to share with me what helped them along the pathway. Don't shy away from meeting as many editors, agents, and freelancers as possible. After all, they are at the conference for you.

In addition, grow your knowledge of the book industry by reading books both in and outside your genre and books on writing. Continue to be a student. Talk with other authors in your writers' groups and ask them about their own discoveries and their journey. Be a voracious reader and learner.

Expand Your Understanding through Writer Conferences

Take it from someone who once stood precisely where you are now, we all start at the beginning, with limited knowledge of what we're about to undertake. That's why the first thing to do is take a step. And a writer's conference is a significant first step. I recall attending my first conference, the Florida Christian Writers' Conference. As I approached the registration desk, someone asked about my "genre." Realizing I had been pronouncing the word incorrectly still brings a smile to my face.

I had already penned a Bible study and a young adult fiction book, yet it was only through attending this conference that I realized how much I had to learn. The art of writing, the rules of grammar, and the strategies for fiction and nonfiction were all uncharted territories. I was a novice, unaware of my lack of knowledge until that moment of awakening at the conference. They say you don't know what you don't know until you know what you don't know.

No one ever published the Bible study and fiction book I wrote, though the Bible study won an award for unpublished works at the Blue Ridge Mountains Christian Writers' Conference. Writing these manuscripts was great practice.

Following my initial conference, I got down to business and created my social media profiles and joined a Christian writers' group. I uploaded the same professional headshot to all my profiles so I was easily recognized from one platform to the next.

I was determined to succeed in this career God was nudging me toward. Your first conference may be an eye-opener, but it will also be the place where your true education as an author begins. Appendix 1 includes how you can get access to a list of Christian writer conferences. For new writers, I recommend attending the Blue Lake Christian Writers Conference (BLCWC.com) because it is a smaller, economical conference with an intimate, healthy living retreat setting where you get to know the faculty.

Besides learning the craft of writing, conferences provide an opportunity to meet other professionals. I met Michelle Medlock Adams at my first conference and attended one of her classes. She was helpful and encouraging. Through the years we became friends. You do not know how a person you meet at a conference may help you in your career or become a friend.

In fact, you will find most if not all the people in the Christian publishing industry to be supportive. They want to help you succeed. Typically they are not competitive. We are all on God's team to further the kingdom of God through the message he placed in our hearts to write. Each message is significant. We should all be obedient to his divine calling.

I created a business card for that first conference, which listed future books I was interested in writing. The list of books included a Daniel young adult book, hospice nonfiction, Star Wars Bible study, parenting book on discipline, and Scripture yoga. One publisher explained that having so many genres was like having split personalities. I needed to choose one and focus on that. At the time, I didn't understand why I couldn't focus on multiple genres.

Create a Professional Business Card

A valuable part of attending writer conferences is the networking opportunity. But once you return home, it's easy to forget to reconnect with the intriguing people you met. Having a business card is crucial for a professional impression and to facilitate future contact. If you want to establish yourself in this career, creating polished business cards is an essential first step.

Your card should have a clean, visually pleasing design that reflects your author brand, if you have established that yet. If you haven't, create a generic business card and print it at home before investing in professional card printing. I did this before attending my first writers' conference. Include your website and email address. Make sure your website includes links to your social media outlets so others can follow you online, or you could include your social media handle on your card. Include a high-quality headshot photo, so others remember you.

If you don't have a professional headshot make plans to get one taken at an upcoming conference. Many offer this opportunity. Treat your author career with professionalism by investing in services like photographers. A friendly portrait goes a long way to connect with publishers, readers, and other authors.

Beyond the standard contact details, consider adding a quick response (QR) code that links to your author website or book trailer video. Or include a brief tagline that hints at your writing genre or style. Small creative touches make your card more intriguing.

Networking is invaluable for authors, but follow-up is key. Business cards enable you to easily swap information, turning those conference conversations into lasting connections. Acquaintances I've met at conferences are the ones who cheer me on when I post on social media about my writing career.

Prepare for a Writers' Conference

It is essential to thoroughly prepare before attending any writers' conference to ensure you get a substantial return on your investment of time and money. Start by reviewing all the classes on the conference website to determine which would be best for you. I print the list of classes and sit outside while I highlight the classes that align with my developmental needs. Some advanced classes may require preregistration, so check early and secure your spots as needed. Create a comprehensive plan of the sessions you intend to attend. It's wise to have this organized beforehand since conferences can be fast-paced and leave little room for last-minute decisions.

At most conferences, you will choose from a list of faculty—publishers, agents, marketers—to schedule one-on-one appointments to present your project. When planning to pitch a book, prepare a one-sheet that introduces you and your book idea in one page, and a book proposal. The proposal should include the first three chapters of your book—or the entire manuscript if it's a children's book. Having these chapters professionally edited beforehand can enhance your presentation.

At the conference appointment, I initially hand the publisher my one-sheet as I smile and look in their eyes. The faculty member can peruse the sheet as I sit down and get settled. You want to take advantage of every second because fifteen minutes goes by quickly. If he or she requests a book proposal for the project you pitched, show how prepared you are by handing them a proposal. That shows the publisher you will do the work necessary to get your book published.

Ensure you arrive on time to faculty appointments. At the time of your appointment, stand a couple of yards away but close enough to maintain visibility with the faculty member to keep the meetings on schedule.

When you choose your faculty appointments, do your research ahead of time. Find out what kind of authors and books their agency or publishing company represent. If you write fiction, you don't want to spend one of your precious appointments with a publisher who doesn't publish novels.

Reference your faculty list when you're at the conference to help you juggle everything you set out to accomplish. Don't try to remember it all. Reviewing your organized lists when you arrive is a lifesaver.

At some conferences you might be able to schedule these one-on-one appointments with other authors. These are invaluable opportunities to pick their brains about the questions you have from your author journey. Be sure to have some questions ready and know what type of books they write. Again, it wouldn't help you much to have time with a novelist when you're writing nonfiction.

Don't miss the opportunity to sit with faculty and other conferees who you'd like to meet, especially if you don't have an appointment with them. The faculty is always accommodating to share mealtimes and get to know you. Also, look for other conferees who may be from your area. This could lead to great friendships or even starting a writers' group in your community.

Many conferences offer the opportunity to submit writing projects for critique. These paid critiques not only provide valuable feedback but also secure additional face-to-face time with faculty members. (Critique appointments are in addition to your allotted faculty appointments.) Choose who will critique your work based on their professional alignment with your project's needs. I strategically choose a publisher, editors, agents, or coaches to critique my work—depending upon my needs.

Participating in conference contests can be highly beneficial. Don't be afraid to enter even as a new writer. Every winner started out just like you. Winning or placing in these contests enhances your credibility as an award-winning author, which can be a significant boost in your bio. Achievements in contests can also attract attention from agents and publishers, potentially leading to representation and publishing opportunities. An agent offered me a contract after I won third place in a conference contest.

Conferences are not just for learning but for cultivating industry relationships too. With each conference, you meet more publishing professionals and gain more contacts. During a conference, be sure to also collect fellow conferees' business cards. When you get home, visit the websites listed on their cards and friend them on each social media network. This is how to build a following. Continue to stay in contact with these incredible individuals you meet. You do not know how another author may positively influence your career.

As authors we need to invest in our career by attending conferences. And we need to prepare for the conference as well. This list should help you plan for any writers' conference:

1. List the classes you plan to attend and register if needed.
2. Create a one-sheet.
3. Complete a book proposal.
4. Create a faculty appointments list and another list of people you want to sit with during a meal.
5. Pay for critiques with several faculty members.
6. Enter your work in the conference contest.
7. Review your lists during the conference.

You invest time and money in attending a conference. Preconference planning helps you get the most value for the money spent.

Write a Book Proposal

Creating a compelling book proposal is crucial for capturing the interest of agents and publishers. This document serves as your pitch, highlighting not only the content of your book but also its marketability and potential success. Start your proposal with a dynamic book description that captures the essence of your work and an engaging author biography that showcases your credentials and personal connection to the topic.

Next, detail your marketing strategy. Outline your target audience and explain how you plan to reach them, including any existing platforms, followers, or networking channels you will use. Highlight plans for promotional activities and how you intend to sustain interest in your book post-launch.

Include a section on endorsements, specifying influential individuals or respected figures in your field who have agreed to endorse your book or whom you plan to approach. This demonstrates to potential publishers the credibility and network potential of your work.

Conduct a comparative analysis of existing books in the same genre or topic area. Identify similar titles and discuss how your book differs, focusing on unique angles, fresh insights, or new contributions to the subject matter. This comparison shows how your book stands out. A well-crafted book proposal is more than just an introduction to your book—it's a strategic tool that conveys your vision, professionalism, and commitment to making your book a success.

Understand Consistency of Genre

If you want to be successful in this career it is best to stick to one genre. If you switch to one with a different readership, then you lose your momentum of establishing a platform, and it is harder to sell your latest book. For example, at this point in my career, I've published nine healthy living books. If I were to publish a novel, only a small portion of my readership would purchase it. However, if my previous reader enjoyed one of my healthy living books, they are more likely to purchase my next book in the same genre. I've already established my nonfiction base of readership. It would be foolish to start all over again developing a new set of readers for a different genre.

Genres go far beyond fiction versus nonfiction. Each of these areas contains a myriad of genres and categories of subject and type. Just peruse the aisles of your favorite bookstore or the category lists on Amazon.

Choosing the right genre can be challenging. It was for me. However, sometimes God might be the one closing some doors and opening others. The writing life surges with rejection. Sometimes we get rejected because we haven't learned the craft. It takes a while to grasp grammar, learn plotting, or appropriately research a topic. Persevering through the ups and downs of this career is key to success.

I tried to write young adult fiction, Chicken Soup stories, Upper Room devotions, and a multitude of magazine articles. I received a rejection letter with everything I tried. However, I read that Stephen King nailed a spike to a wall and hung each rejection letter on the spike. That gave me hope, so I kept writing.

Year after year, I continued to hone my craft. I attended my writers' group and writers' conferences. I pitched my book ideas to publishers and agents, all to no avail. Finally, I self-published. My first two books sold very few copies.

Nevertheless, I kept trying because I felt spiritually led to pursue this career. One day I got the idea to write a book to help others quit eating sugar and refined carbohydrates. I intertwined my personal story of how I lost and regained my health and my sister's story of getting off sugar and gluten into the book 7 *Steps to Get Off Sugar and Carbohydrates*. This is the book that sells a thousand copies a month. Once I completed it, I submitted it to the Selah Awards contest at the Blue Ridge Mountains Christian Writers Conference and won first place in the Christian living category. Receiving this award gave it a wonderful marketing boost.

Suddenly, the doors of opportunity opened. Magazines published my health-related articles instead of rejecting them. A dream came true when my interview on Christian Television Network's *Bridges* show aired across the nation.

All those years of rejection ultimately led to a path where I could use my nursing background and my own heartfelt experience to help others regain their health. My writers' group also helped me understand I should write nonfiction Christian books focused on healthy living since I am a registered nurse with a master's in health science and a health nut. This genre makes perfect sense. The Bible study and young adult fiction did not. I believe many of the rejections I received during my career have kept me focused on God's divine writing plan for me.

I am finally pursuing a divine direction, but it took me years to figure it out. I wasn't supposed to be a fiction or devotional author; I was supposed to use my background to assist others with health issues. I encountered much rejection along the way, but I continued to persevere.

Have you determined the spiritual writing path you should pursue? If not, allow me to mentor you through coaching (susanuneal.com/author-coaching-packages-with-susan-neal) or attend the Blue Lake Christian Writers Conference and set up a mentoring appointment with me.

Romans 5:3–5 inspires us, "We can rejoice, too, when we run into problems and trials, for we know that they help us develop endurance. And endurance develops strength of character, and character strengthens our confident hope of salvation. And this hope will not lead to disappointment. For we know how dearly God loves us, because he has given us the Holy Spirit to fill our hearts with his love" (NLT).

Be a Voracious Reader of the Craft

Like any art, writing has its tools and techniques that, when understood, will elevate your work tremendously. In addition to attending conferences, begin reading books about the writing craft. I recommend *Proofreading Secrets of Best-Selling Authors* by Kathy Ide. I used to sprinkle commas with a liberal hand, not fully grasping their proper place. Determined to conquer this, I delved into grammatical guides and texts, and learned the rules of punctuation. Through persistence and study, I changed from a novice to being affectionately dubbed the "comma queen" by my peers. This transformation is a testament to the growth we can achieve when we commit to learning. And learning is great for our brains!

Don't forget the novels and stories that fall within your chosen realm of writing. To read is to fill your mind with a wealth of examples and styles that define your genre. Each book is a lesson, revealing subtleties of pacing, character development, and plot that you can weave into your own writing tapestry.

Embrace this journey with an eagerness to learn and a willingness to grow. As you do, you'll find your voice growing stronger, your skills sharper, and your place within the literary world more assured. We learn, we grow, and indeed, we succeed.

Build a Social Media Platform

To help you increase your social media following, request business cards from everyone you meet at writer conferences. Tell them you plan to send them a friend request on social media. I used this method to increase my followers, and I have stayed in touch with many writers I've met through social media. These followers respond to my posts about my writing career. They get excited for me with each success in my profession. We can be encouragers for each other in this writing career.

Personally, I dislike social media. Most authors do. However, social media is a powerful business tool for authors. Yet not everyone uses it effectively. Over the years, I've worked on improving my reach and engagement on Facebook, X (previously known as Twitter), LinkedIn, Instagram, YouTube, and Pinterest. However, it is best for an author to choose two social media platforms. Otherwise you could spend all your time on these sites instead of writing. To help you decide which platforms to focus on, figure out where your target audience hangs out. Most of my readers congregate on Facebook, so I use this site most.

We live in a pay-to-play digital world. These social media platforms expect you to pay them to show your post to more of your followers. And that works well for some. But it is time-consuming, tedious, and expensive. Especially since it is difficult to find our Christian market on Facebook. I've had a hard time posting enticing Facebook ads since many of my ads promote optimal health and weight.

However, I discovered several tactics to get Facebook to show my posts without paying them. Before publishing each book, I post two versions of the book cover and ask followers to vote on their preferred one. Asking them to vote on a book title also works well. People enjoy providing their opinion, so ask them for their feedback. Facebook shows these posts to lots of followers because the comments and votes positively activate Facebook's algorithm.

To stimulate the algorithm further, remark on each comment, but do more than say, "Thanks." Ask them a question. For example, to a fellow author I may respond to their comment by saying, "It was great to see you at the Blue Lake Christian Writers Conference last year. Will you be attending next month?"

Engagement is exactly what most social media sites want. So give it to them. Always respond to someone commenting on your post and ask them a corresponding question. I found this technique to be much better than paying this social media platform for an ad.

The platform I found the most success with, other than Facebook, was Pinterest. I will share this process in the next chapter in hopes that you will learn how to increase your website views by using Pinterest.

Summary

Overall, as a new author, attending writers' conferences and building your network is crucial for gaining knowledge and making connections in the publishing industry. Seek mentors and join Christian writing groups to continue honing your craft.

Choose your genre thoughtfully based on your skills, interests, and audience. Use social media strategically to build your author platform. Ensure you gain knowledge about the writing craft through reading books. With dedication to learning the craft and business of writing, you can find success and meaningfully influence lives through your words.

Action Steps

1. Review different writer conferences and register for one that fits your needs.

2. Create a business card to share at the conference with other attendees.
3. Schedule to get a headshot if you don't have one yet.
4. Make a comprehensive preconference plan.
5. Create a one-sheet and possibly a book proposal to give to publishers or agents at a conference.
6. Figure out your best writing genre and stick to it.
7. Read writing-craft books to improve your prose.
8. Read books in the genre you write in.
9. Build your social media platform by friending other authors.
10. Choose two social media sites that you will primarily focus on.

Chapter 5

Master Search Engine Results through Blogging, Keywords, and Categories

You've invested in crafting a website and publishing a book, but those endeavors alone won't automatically attract website visitors. How do you get people to visit your website? Strategic blogging is the answer. Creating consistent blogs is one of the most effective tactics to generate fresh site content that appeals to search engines, but also creates new points of entry to attract your target readers.

Each new blog post acts as another opportunity to increase your ranking on a search engine and your perceived authority in your field. Then more people who are attracted to your brand can find you. This chapter will teach you everything you need to know to drive more traffic to your website.

Driving Website Traffic: The Power of Strategic Blogging

We know that people endlessly go to search engines for answers on needs or questions in their lives. But most people don't scroll past the first page for those answers. If you look at the bottom of your search page, you'll notice thousands of potential clicks to find the information you seek. How do you get your author page to rank higher on these search engine pages?

First you need to understand how search engines work and how to maximize them for your benefit. Blogs are a great way to influence search engines. If you want blogging to increase your website traffic, it requires knowledge of how search engine optimization (SEO) works. Here are some effective ways to write blogs that may increase your SEO rank and drive more traffic to your website.

- Study keyword research to uncover high-traffic terms you can naturally weave into your blog content. These keywords are those your reader is most likely to use in a search.
- Optimize your titles, headers, meta descriptions (the brief description that appears under a search option), and image titles for improved ranking.
- Create links between your posts and your website pages to reinforce a topic that you want to rank highly on your website.
- Distribute share-friendly social media content to amplify your posts' visibility.

These SEO techniques increase your website's visitor rate. Embrace the power of blogging and start driving traffic to your website. However, when approached purposefully, a blog serves as more than just an SEO tool—it's a vibrant content stage for sharing insights, personal stories, and magnifying your brand's overall message to help your readers.

The first step is to create a theme for your blog by determining your blog's three-to-five keywords you would like to use for ranking on Google (or any search engine). (See the Keywords and Categories section later in this chapter.)

For example, the primary keywords for my Healthy Living Series blog (SusanUNeal.com/healthy-living-blog) are *low-sugar diet, low-*

carb diet, gluten-free, Candida, and *food addiction.* Secondary keywords include *healthy diet, healthy lifestyle,* and *healthy eating.* I want my blogs to come up on the first page of an internet search when one of these keywords are used, so I repeat them in my blogs. After some time, the internet search engine (Google, Safari, etc.) recognizes my site as an authority on these topics.

Create engaging blog titles to lure the customer to your website. Solve your customer's problem in your title. Here are some examples: How to, 5 Ways to, Avoid These Mistakes, and Client Success Story.

Use the Advanced Marketing Institute's headline analyzer at aminstitute.com/headline. This free tool analyzes your headline to see how someone might emotionally react to it. Reaching readers in a deep emotional way is key to successful copywriting. Try to get a score of forty or more.

For each blog you write, make sure the first two lines tell readers what the blog is about and how it will benefit them. These first two sentences are what show up on an internet search. They are called the blog's metadata. You must hook the viewer so they will click on your blog's brief description and visit your website. If the first two sentences do not clearly define what the article is about and how it will benefit the reader, you lost your potential customer.

When using images in blogs, be sure to title the graphic in a way that describes what it is. For example, I've titled a microscopic photo of the yeast candida with its formal name *Albicans Candida.* Since search engine bots cannot see what is on the image, each uploaded blog photo should include a descriptive title. Consequently, my blog ranks higher as a knowledge source for this microbe.

When you fuse captivating writing that provides authentic value to your readers, along with intentional, SEO-minded blogging, your website becomes a powerful lead-generation mechanism. Each new post increases your digital real estate, affording more entry points for audiences to discover and become engrossed in your literary world.

Driving traffic to your website is vital to your success as an author. But how often should you post a new blog? Weekly is best, but at least twice a month. Keeping up a weekly blog requires a significant amount of work. Therefore, I ask other writers for guest submissions. Create blog guidelines for them to follow, include adding your blog's pertinent keywords you want them to include in their submission, so your website ranks for them on the internet search engine.

Use Pinterest Pins in Your Blogs

Another way I increased my website's (SusanUNeal.com) search views was by adding three visually appealing Pinterest pins to my blogs. I hired a social media strategist to manage my account. She uses the social media scheduler Tailwind to post my blog's new pins to my Pinterest page regularly. This platform wants you to do more than merely pin other people's pins; they want you to create new pins and idea pins. And when you do, your account will benefit from their algorithm.

Pinterest is also a search engine, and a superb social media platform. For those of you who are artistic, you can create your own pins on Canva.com. It takes a creative person to design visually appealing graphics. Some people have that talent, others do not. That's why I hired a graphic designer to create mine.

Coming up with strong keywords for the title of your pin is also crucial. Use your book's and blog's keywords. (See the Keywords and Categories section later in this chapter.)

I increase my website views by writing blogs specific to current issues and creating corresponding pins. People click on my pins within Pinterest, which boosts traffic to my website. In fact, I found Pinterest to be more effective at driving traffic to my website than all my other social media platforms combined.

To discover trending blog topics, go to your Pinterest account and click on the search bar. A drop-down menu appears with the following categories: "Ideas for You" and "Popular on Pinterest." You could write a new blog on one of these topics.

We only have so much time, so we need to figure out which techniques work best. Pinterest was the top social media winner for me. If you haven't invested time in managing your account and added beautifully designed pins to your blogs, I suggest you start now. By focusing on this platform, my book sales soared. If you're looking for a Pinterest strategist, see appendix 1. If you need additional blogging guidance, see the course Blogging to Drive Traffic to Your Website at CIPA.Podia.com.

Determine Strong Keywords

Determine your book's corresponding keywords—words and phrases that describe your book's topic and benefits. But not just any words will do. You want keywords that are searched by thousands of people monthly on Amazon. To find highly searched keywords, use Publisher Rocket. This software shows you the monthly search volume for each keyword on Amazon, so you can select those with the highest search volume. If you want to be strategic and sell more books, this software is indispensable. (See appendix 1 to learn how to receive 30 percent off Publisher Rocket and where you can find a professional to determine your book's categories and keywords.)

Amazon allows you to list seven keywords for the ebook and another seven for the print book. That's fourteen keywords, not just seven. Determining the highest searched keywords will help your book rank well on Amazon. You can add more than one keyword per line on KDP.com if a comma and space separate them. For example—*low-carb diet, healthy eating, Candida*—can be put on one keyword line (that's three keyword phrases instead of one). So you or your publisher can add over fourteen keywords.

At the time I chose the keywords for my book *Solving the Gluten Puzzle*, over eighteen thousand readers searched for those words on Amazon monthly. I also added these keywords into the book's description. Amazon needs information about a book to get it into the appropriate readers' hands, and using keywords is how to give it to them.

Choose Strategic Categories

Amazon uses categories to rank books. Typically, your book is placed in three Amazon categories. When choosing categories, be sure they match the content in your book. Categories are like genres. If you strategically choose categories with less competition, your book ranking can increase and get on an Amazon bestseller list. This should be a goal for any author.

My book 7 *Steps to Get Off Sugar and Carbohydrates* typically ranks in one or two of Amazon's bestseller lists. I chose the category healthy diet over diet because it is more specific with fewer competitive books. Many times this book will rank number one in a category. When your book ranks as a number-one bestseller, Amazon posts a bestseller sticker next to the book on its product page. Now that is advertising at its best, and it is free!

Figuring out book categories can be challenging as there are thousands of categories for both ebooks and print books. Therefore, I recommend you purchase the software program Publisher Rocket mentioned earlier, which identifies the best keywords and categories for your book.

Besides writing a book and marketing it, an author must understand search engines and Amazon and use all the technological strategies to rank high on these sites. There is a science to getting your book to rank and sell well. If we understand what we need to do, we can do it. That's what this book is all about. It teaches you the nuances of these sites and how to make them work to your advantage.

One year while I was teaching a practicum at a writers' conference about expanding your books' categories and keywords, my book 7 *Steps to Get Off Sugar and Carbohydrates* ranked number one in the Candida category. And my second book in the series, *Christian*

Study Guide for 7 Steps to Get Off Sugar and Carbohydrates, ranked number five in this same category.

My class was amazed to see my books received such high Amazon ranks. One attendee commented, "Expanding your book's categories and keywords really works." Yes, it does!

Choosing the right keywords and categories is crucial to optimizing your book's visibility and discoverability on Amazon. Conduct thorough research using tools like Publisher Rocket to identify keywords with high search volume and categories with less competition where your book can rise in rankings.

Precise categorization and strategic keyword selection enable Amazon's algorithm to correctly match your book with searching readers. It takes time and effort to implement these changes, but it will help more people discover, read about, and buy your book. With the proper building blocks of highly searched keywords and well-chosen categories, you can unlock your book's sales potential.

Summary

In today's digital landscape, the role of an author extends far beyond simply crafting a book and promoting it. Navigating the intricate world of search engines and platforms like Amazon has become essential. To truly thrive, authors must develop a comprehensive grasp of the technological strategies and algorithms that govern online discoverability and sales rankings. There is a science behind elevating a book's visibility and performance on these critical platforms. It requires a willingness to embrace continuous learning and adapting strategies as the digital platforms evolve.

The central mission of this book is to empower authors with that vital knowledge base. In this chapter we reviewed how to get your website to rank on search engines and your book on digital retail systems like Amazon. You are learning how to use technology intentionally to position your book optimally within this modern marketplace. Armed with these specialized techniques, you can expertly capitalize on the opportunities these platforms offer to enhance your book's success.

Action Steps

1. Blog to drive traffic to your website.
2. Learn about the SEO techniques to use in your blogs.
3. Take the course Blogging to Drive Traffic to Your Website at CIPA.Podia.com.
4. Purchase the software program Publisher Rocket to help you identify the best keywords for your blog and book as well as your book's best Amazon categories.
5. Define your website's keywords you want to rank for on search engines.
6. Sprinkle those keywords into your blogs and blog titles.
7. Add Pinterest pins to each blog and pin them on your Pinterest boards.
8. Determine your book's keywords and incorporate them into your book's title, subtitle, and description.
9. Identify your books categories with less competition where your book can rise in Amazon ranking.
10. Take the course Improve Your Book's Amazon Rank through Expanding Categories and Strengthening Keywords at CIPA.Podia.com.

Chapter 6

Navigate the Publishing Journey: Traditional versus Self-Publishing

Should you traditionally publish or self-publish? Some authors can't land a traditional publishing contract, so that is not an alternative. Since the pandemic, it has become even more challenging to get a publishing contract. Other authors are traditionally published and could continue be, but they are curious about self-publishing. They may get frustrated about specific aspects of the traditional world.

On the other hand, while self-publishing used to have an amateur reputation, the increase in the options for independently publishing your book have created many more avenues for authors who strike out on their own. Some authors eventually publish both traditionally and independently, depending on the book and the circumstances. So how does a new author determine the best path to take?

Perks of Traditional Publishing

Some aspects remain the same with self-publishing or traditional publishing. The author needs to write a well-written, interesting book and is responsible for marketing it. When you work with a traditional publisher, you do not incur the costs associated with publishing a book. However, after publication, you do not have control over it (fixing editing errors, choosing the cover and title, putting the book on sale, and changing Amazon categories). Some authors find that frustrating.

Traditional publishing has its perks, as you do not have to worry about all the nitty-gritty phases of preparing your book for publication. Publishers request your input at pertinent points during the publishing process, but otherwise, you do not have to coordinate all the aspects of getting your book published, such as the book cover and formatting. However, as a traditionally published author, you share a substantial amount of your profits.

When negotiating a contract with a traditional publisher, it's advisable to have a literary agent represent you. Agents typically take a 15 percent commission from your book profits, but they often justify this by getting better contract terms and higher payments. You won't have any upfront costs for their services. A friend hired an agent after receiving a publishing offer, as she felt unprepared to understand and negotiate the terms on her own. When attending writer conferences, schedule appointments with literary agents to explore if they would be interested in representing you.

Some parts of the contract may require clarification, modification, or removal. For instance, in one of my traditional publishing contracts, I requested the removal of a clause that obligated me to publish my next book with the same publisher. You can negotiate additional items into the contract to boost your book's visibility. I asked a publisher to run Amazon ads for the first three months after the book's publication, pay for a book blogger tour, and provide two hundred extra books for distribution at several trade shows. These free copies would be given to attendees such as media, retailers, and churches. Furthermore, ensure your contract includes the provision for the publisher to send copies to influencers and endorsers who can help promote the book.

Another big difference between self-publishing and traditional publishing is the timing of sales reports. Traditional publishers typically provide sales data to authors with a delay of at least three months. In contrast, self-published authors can access sales reports immediately through their publishing platforms. This delay can make it challenging for traditionally published authors to assess the effectiveness of their marketing strategies in real time.

Pros and Cons of Self-Publishing

Initially, self-publishing was seen as inferior. Now, successful traditionally published authors have turned to self-publishing so they don't have to share their profits. Furthermore, they are in control of the process and can publish a book much quicker. Because they own their book and its content, they are protected from arbitrary decisions a publisher might make, such as stopping the printing of the book. However, the author of a self-published title must coordinate all the aspects of creating a professional-looking book.

Advantages
The author:

- receives all the profits.
- controls the publishing timeline.
- can edit their manuscript if they find an error after publication.
- can edit a book cover or add an award emblem after publication.
- can put their books on sale for special promotions.
- owns their book rights.

Disadvantages
The author:

- does not have the resources and guidance of a traditional publisher.
- has to hire an editor, proofreader, cover designer, and book formatter or do it themselves.
- must learn the publishing steps.
- need funds to purchase the International Standard Book Number (ISBN) and pay for other services.

If you are a seasoned author who understands the publishing process and has the financial resources to publish a book, it might be prudent to try self-publishing. If you don't like it, go back to traditional publishing. I know successful authors who are hybrid published. They have many books published by traditional publishers. But when a traditional publisher rejects a manuscript, they self-publish.

I could not land a publishing contract for my first book, *Scripture Yoga*. I pitched my proposal to several publishers at a couple of Christian writers' conferences. I prayed and felt God leading me to publish this book, so I joined Christian Book Academy (ChristianBookAcademy.com) and learned how to self-publish.

Now let's look at the intricacies of self-publishing so if you choose this route, you know what you're getting into.

Navigating Self-Publishing Platforms

The book publishing platforms for uploading and distributing self-published books include:

- Amazon KDP (Kindle Direct Publishing): Amazon's platform to publish ebooks and paperbacks sold on Amazon.com and Kindle. This platform is easy to use. You can choose to have your books only published on Amazon or you can select expanded distribution for massive distribution by KDP.

- IngramSpark: A platform to publish print books and ebooks and distribute them to thousands of retailers like Amazon, Barnes & Noble, bookstores, and libraries. IngramSpark provides more distribution reach than just Amazon but requires a little more setup work.
- Draft2Digital: Specializes in publishing and distributing ebooks to major ebook retailers like Amazon, Apple Books, and Kobo. Draft2Digital simplifies the process of wide ebook distribution and publishes print books.
- Smashwords: A publishing and distribution platform focused on independent authors. Distributes to major retailers and provides free publishing tools.
- Lulu: Print and ebook self-publishing services. Offers publishing tutorials and tools to create the files for print books or ebooks.
- Blurb: Print-on-demand self-publishing platform to create print books and ebooks. Blurb has a reputation for beautiful book designs.

Choosing the right platform depends on your book format needs, distribution goals, and technical skills. Christian Book Academy included a course that showed me how to input all my book's metadata into KDP. I used that course to toggle back and forth from the course to KDP to publish my book.

Gathering all your book's metadata makes this process easier. (See appendix 1 for a Checklist for Book Metadata.) Publishing is like riding a bike; learning is difficult, but once you've published one or two books, it's easier but still requires work.

Evaluate each platform to find the best fit for you and your needs. I publish on two platforms: KDP and IngramSpark. First, I publish my ebook on KDP under the KDP Select program, which allows me to automate my ebook sale every three months. (If not on KDP Select, you can still put your book on sale whenever you want, but you have to do it manually.)

Next I publish my print book on KDP, but I do *not* click expanded distribution. This selection does not allow KDP to put my book into other retailers like Barnes & Noble. If you give KDP the expanded distribution rights to your book, when you try to publish on another platform like IngramSpark, they will ask for another ISBN for your book. If this occurs, go back and remove the expanded distribution selection on KDP, and wait for KDP to perform that request before trying to republish on another platform. You should not have to use two ISBNs for your book.

Next, I publish my print book only on IngramSpark. I had very few ebook sales through Ingram, so I publish my ebook only on KDP Select. While publishing on IngramSpark, I select for this platform to distribute my books to retailers. I offer a 45–55 percent discount off the retail price and allow the books to be returnable. These two selections are necessary if you want to entice retailers to carry your books.

Christian bookstores do not purchase their books from Amazon because it is too expensive, and Amazon is their major competitor. Christian retailers buy from Ingram, Anchor Distributors, and Spring Arbor Distributors. Spring Arbor is the distributor for IngramSpark.

To get your book carried in this Christian distributor, your book must have a Christian Book Industry Standard & Communications (BISAC) code. Additionally, you need to request IngramSpark to carry your book in Spring Arbor. This step ensures your books can be carried in Christian bookstores.

While traditional publishers handle editing, design, and marketing in-house, they use these distributors like Ingram and Baker & Taylor for warehousing and wholesaling physical books to retailers.

Securing an ISBN

A self-published author needs to purchase their International Standard Book Numbers (ISBNs), which are unique thirteen-digit codes that identify published books. Each version of your book (print, hardcover, audiobook, etc.) requires a separate ISBN. The ISBN appears on the back cover and the copyright page of your book.

An ISBN acts like a product barcode so that stores and libraries can identify your book. Many online publishing platforms like Amazon's Kindle Direct Publishing (KDP) will provide you a free ISBN, but it ties your book exclusively to their platform. You do not want to use another platform's ISBN. Purchasing your own ISBN allows you to distribute your book more widely and maintain your ownership, which is preferred.

You can buy single ISBNs, but it is more cost effective to purchase them in bulk (ten, one hundred, or one thousand ISBNs) from an official ISBN agency like Bowker (MyIdentifiers.com). Having your own ISBNs allows maximum visibility and credibility for your self-published books. Investing in them upfront is well worth it for your career as an indie author. (See appendix 1 for more information about ISBN discounts.)

Creating a Professional Imprint and Managing Business Financials

A publishing imprint is your publishing company name or brand. As a self-publisher, creating your own imprint establishes you as an official publisher and gives your books a professional, unified identity. Choose a memorable, meaningful imprint title. It can be your ministry name or a creative business name representing you or your values. Next, create an imprint logo to use when publishing your books. Designating your publishing imprint and establishing consistent use of it and your own ISBNs across all books gives you a professional brand.

I created a limited liability corporation (LLC) using the name Christian Indie Publishing, and had my graphic designer create a logo for the imprint. Creating a separate checking account and credit card keeps all my business transactions separate. I've used Quick-Books for over a decade to enter my monthly revenue and expenses.

For tax purposes, it is easy to print a Profit and Loss statement for my accountant.

Crafting the Perfect Cover

Readers typically see your book cover first, so it must make a great impression. As a self-publisher, you get to design your own cover rather than relying on your publisher's in-house designers. This creative freedom is exciting but also challenging.

Unless you have artistic talent, invest in a quality freelance cover designer familiar with industry standards because you need to adhere to retailer requirements for spine width, bleed, color space, etc. A book cover (front and back) must include specific elements—author name, book title and subtitle, price, barcode with ISBN, and BISAC code. Professional designers understand and meet these requirements. However, KDP and IngramSpark provide cover templates for you to use to create your own, if you choose.

Craft a title and subtitle that are intriguing yet clearly convey your subject, and incorporate keywords that readers search for on Amazon. Perform a title search on Amazon and Christian Book Distributors (christianbook.com) to ensure you don't duplicate a title you do not want to be associated with. Book titles are not eligible for copyright protection. So you can use a previously published book title if you want.

A book cover should be visually pleasing yet stand out at the same time. Check your book's thumbnail version to ensure you can see the image and read the title. Light backgrounds with dark text tend to show up best.

The cover needs to grab a reader's interest. Ask trusted readers and authors for input on cover concepts before finalizing. Be sure to post two versions of the cover on social media and let your audience vote on them. This tactic always gives me a lot of traffic on Facebook, and I don't have to pay them to get my desired engagement.

A striking cover conveys your book's essence, fits your genre, and attracts your target audience. Invest time and money into this vital marketing piece and bring your story to life.

Don't forget the back cover too. This may be the second place a potential reader looks to determine whether to invest in your book. Your cover designer will also create the back cover and spine, but you will provide them with the content. In back cover content, you'll want to match the needs of the reader to the message of your book with a marketing-style approach. You might ask yourself: what do I want my reader to gain by reading this book? You'll also need to provide a short author bio and photo to place on the back cover.

Determining Keywords, Amazon Categories, and BISAC Codes

Keywords, categories, and BISAC codes are critical metadata (book information) that help readers discover your book. All authors need to ensure they optimize these elements. Brainstorm words and phrases readers would use to search for your book. Use keyword research tools like Publisher Rocket and Google AdWords to identify high-volume, low-competition terms. Take the time to determine the most highly searched keywords to input into the publishing platform you or your publisher uses. (See appendix 1 for my course Determine Your Book's Most Strategic Categories & Strongest Keywords.)

When you use highly searched keywords, it makes it easier for readers to find your book when browsing and searching on Amazon and bookstore websites and in physical bookstores. Incorporate those keywords into the book's title, subtitle, description, and within the text to boost search visibility.

There is more to publishing than simply writing a book. For your book to get maximum discoverability, authors must learn about search engine optimization (see chapter 5). I enjoy figuring out how to manage IngramSpark, Amazon, Facebook, and Google. Authors need to learn what these platforms require from us as users and follow their procedures. If we do, we can use these companies to our advantage. By diligently studying and implementing tactics and best practices, authors can increase exposure, improve rankings, and heighten book sales. We simply need to understand their systems and what we need to do—that's what I love to teach.

Amazon organizes books in categories to connect with the right readers. You can choose up to three categories. Analyze options on Publisher Rocket to find less competitive categories that still fit your book. Chapter 5 discussed this topic in further detail.

Authors also need to understand BISAC codes, which provide industry-approved alphanumeric codes assigned to topical book subject headings. Basically, it's a book category. For example, young adult fiction and biography and autobiography are BISAC codes. BISAC codes categorize books by genre/topic.

A BISAC code on the back of your book tells the bookstore which section of the store to place your book. Publishers and independent authors upload one to two codes into the IngramSpark publishing platform. Choose codes that accurately reflect your content for proper shelf placement.

Polishing Your Manuscript

A professional editor and proofreader should edit all published books. As a self-published author, I needed to find an editor, so I contacted the chair of a large Christian writers' conference and asked who she recommended. She referred me to an excellent nonfiction editor and my book *7 Steps to Get Off Sugar and Carbohydrates* won the Selah Award. After formatting my book, I hired several people to proofread it.

Even in traditional publishing, while publishers provide editing, design, and production services, authors play an integral role in reviewing and approving key stages. Carefully examine edited manuscripts and formatted book pages and proofread them carefully. Errors always slip through, so extra scrutiny is critical. Catching and fixing mistakes before publication improves quality and gives your book the polish required to potentially win awards.

After publishing your book, most traditional publishers will not fix errors. This is a notable difference between self-publishing and the traditional route.

Don't take a hands-off approach with your publisher. Treat it like a partnership. Stay engaged in each phase, provide feedback, and verify everything is flawless. A friend did not engage in the proofreading process of her traditionally published book, and they formatted the book as a fiction book. (Fiction books have chapters start on the page immediately following a previous chapter, whereas nonfiction books generally start each chapter on the right side of a book page after a previous chapter ends.) So her book was shorter than it should have been. Another friend had her book endorsement page missing, but the publisher would not go back and add it, even though it was their oversight. Your involvement in the publishing process upholds excellence, and an active partnership leads to publishing success.

Compose Your Front and Back Matter

Crafting a professional book requires understanding what elements belong in the front and back matter. If you choose to self-publish, educate yourself on industry standards for these components.

The front matter comes before the core text and can include:

- title page with book title and author name
- copyright page with ISBN, publisher, and publication date
- dedication page
- table of contents
- foreword (written by someone else)
- preface (written by the author)

The back matter follows the core text and may include:

- appendices with supplementary information
- glossary defining key terms
- endnotes
- bibliography and references
- index
- about the author section
- additional books by the author

Format your front and back matter properly to give your book a polished, credible appearance. Consult publishing guides and courses to master the nuances. If you want to self-publish a professional book, take the course How to Create a Professional-Looking Book at CIPA.Podia.com. Treat your self-published book with the same care as a traditional release.

Protecting Your Work through Copyrighting

Technically, the copyright symbol and your name automatically copyright your book. However, you can register your legal ownership as the creator of your book if you want to assure you can take legal action if someone violates your copyright. Registering your self-published book is easy:

- Go to the US Copyright Office website at copyright.gov.
- Complete the application form for a literary work, providing your name, book title, year, and other metadata information.
- Upload an electronic copy of your manuscript in PDF format or mail in a physical copy. This verifies your authorship.
- Pay the registration fee, typically $55 for an ebook or paperback.

In a few months, you will receive an official registration letter and certificate of registration documenting your copyright. Your book is now protected under copyright law. Include the copyright notice (© Your Name, Year) on the copyright page, whether or not you register the book. Copyright law protects your work if someone uses it without permission. It also gives you credibility as an official published author. The straightforward process is inexpensive peace of mind for any self-publisher. Traditional publishers typically do this for you.

Formatting the Book

Now that you have had your book professionally edited and the cover designed, it is time to format your book. There are several options for formatting:

1. Look for websites or YouTube videos that show you how to format your book in Word and create a PDF file for your print book and an ePub file for your ebook.
2. Use KDP.com's formatting option.
3. Hire a professional formatter.
4. Purchase one of these formatting software products—for a Mac, use Vellum, or for a PC, use Atticus. With a little training, you can format your own book.

I use Vellum. Another popular program used to format is Atticus. I had about three hours of training and found Vellum easy to use. After you publish two books, you've paid for this software program. And you can easily edit your book. Every time I publish a new book, I edit my previous book's Vellum file and add my latest book to the back matter. That's a very effective way for your readers to find your new products. Traditional publishers do not do this.

Whichever process you choose, make sure you understand some basics about how a book's interior should look by perusing your own bookshelf at home to see what book formatting entails. Look to see how different books utilize white space, page numbers, and headings.

Now that you have completed these steps, you can upload your files to a self-publishing platform. I use KDP.com (Amazon) and IngramSpark. Both are easy to use. Choose any of the publishing platforms listed earlier in this chapter (Draft2Digital, IngramSpark, etc.). The platform will instruct you to enter the title, subtitle, author, ISBN, categories, keywords, and retail price. Then, upload the book cover and book files (PDF or ePub). Once you load all the information, you can publish it, but I recommend ordering several proof author copies first. I distribute those copies to my paid proofreaders. As they find errors, I edit the book's Vellum file and recreate a new ePub and PDF file to upload to KDP.com and IngramSpark. I then publish the edited book.

Determine Your Book's Retail Price

Setting the right retail price for your book is crucial for balancing attractiveness to buyers and profitability. To start, research approximately a dozen books that are similar in content, genre, and target audience to yours. Make sure these books are from comparable publishers or are self-published titles with similar production quality.

When gathering your data, exclude any titles with prices that are unusually high or low, as these could skew your average and might not reflect standard market conditions. Add the prices of the remaining books and calculate their average. This average will give you a competitive price point that aligns with current market trends and expectations for books like yours.

Additionally, consider factors such as your book's length, the cost of production, and any unique selling points that might allow for a higher price tag. For instance, if your book includes additional resources like downloadable content, workshops, or exclusive access to online communities, you might justify a slightly higher price.

Finally, think about your own goals: Are you looking to maximize profits, or is broader distribution more important to you? Your pricing strategy should reflect your priorities, whether that means pricing competitively to gain market share or setting a premium price to reflect the high value and unique content of your book.

Establish Your Amazon Author Profile

For independently published authors, creating and maintaining an Amazon Author Central profile is a must. This free service enhances your visibility and credibility with Amazon's readers. Your profile includes your professional author bio, headshot photo, and a list of all your published books. Setting up your profile is simple at AuthorCentral.Amazon.com.

When readers view any of your Amazon book listings, they can click on your name to be taken directly to this curated page summarizing your background and full body of work. When you publish a new book, go to your account and add the book title to your profile. This platform keeps all your published books together under one hub.

Author Central also provides valuable reports listing your number of Amazon followers, book sales rank history, and Bookscan sales report. This reporting information can help you evaluate the impact of your marketing efforts to make informed decisions.

For advanced advertising, a publisher or a self-published author can upload Amazon A+ Content to their book's Amazon page via Author Central. The book-branded graphic, which is located midway down the page, entices the reader to purchase the book. The consumer is already on your book's page, all they need is a little nudge to induce them to invest in the book. To find more information about Amazon A+ Content see appendix 1.

As you can tell, there is a lot to learn about independent publishing. If you like to learn and control all the aspects of your book, you will enjoy it. If you choose the self-publishing route, I recommend joining the Christian Indie Publishing Association at ChristianPublishers.net. This organization, founded in 2004, helps self-published authors publish like a professional. Why do it alone when you can join this association, which provides educational resources and discounts to make your publishing experience easier and more profitable? If you need help through the self-publishing process, see my coaching services at SusanUNeal.com.

After your book is published, if you still find errors, as an indie author you can always correct your mistakes and upload a new version. You retain total control over your book. That is something a traditionally published author cannot do.

Summary

Self-publishing gives authors more control and higher royalties, but requires learning the publishing process and hiring professionals. If you have the motivation to manage your book's production and marketing, it can be rewarding. Seek mentors and education to publish professionally. With dedication and hard work, you can successfully share your message while retaining creative and financial ownership.

While self-publishing has its challenges, the freedom and profits can make it worthwhile for the right author. In fact, some traditionally published authors choose to self-publish after they have established their readership, so they can glean the financial rewards. But they need to learn the publishing steps and industry standards to produce a quality book.

Use resources like editors, formatters, coaches, and author groups. The learning curve is steep, but once mastered, you can reap the benefits of being an independent author. Stay persistent and have faith and grit in your writing journey. Believe in your skills. With dedication and support, you can successfully self-publish!

Action Steps

1. When negotiating a traditionally published book contract, have a literary agent represent you. Negotiate additional terms to boost your books visibility.
2. Research self-publishing platforms, like Kindle Direct Publishing and IngramSpark. Compare their features to determine which fits your book best, or publish on both.
3. Purchase an ISBN. To receive a discount see appendix 1.
4. Choose a memorable, meaningful imprint title, and create an imprint logo.
5. Establish a separate checking account and credit card for your business. Use an accounting software such as QuickBooks.
6. Determine your book's keywords, Amazon categories, and BISAC codes.
7. Create a book cover and format your book's interior.
8. To learn the intricacies of self-publishing, take the course How to Publish a Professional-Looking Book at CIPA.Podia.com.
9. Copyright your book.
10. Set up your Amazon author profile.

Chapter 7

Plan a Successful Book Launch

Now that you've written your manuscript, polished it with professional editing, and enveloped it inside a beautiful cover, it's time to deliver your book to the world. What a glorious day! But launching a book is like giving birth—it takes a lot of work. To ensure a successful launch, it's critical to prepare months in advance before the book's publication date. Many of these suggestions need to be completed up to six months prior to your book's launch.

Much like planning a big party, you'll need to prepare ahead of time. Your launch may be virtual or live or both, and will involve everything from influencers to invitations/evites to marketing. Even if you decide to have a live launch party with friends and family, you'll also need to introduce your book to the larger online publishing community.

Like every other step in your author journey, don't be intimidated at the prospect of a launch. Just as you have prepared for other steps, you can create a plan for a great launch. It's a celebration of a major accomplishment and an introduction of your message to the world!

Secure Beta Readers

Beta readers play a crucial role in helping authors identify problems in their books before its release. Fixing issues that beta readers catch can make the difference between a book being a great seller or a poor one. Beta readers are not editors. They are simply people who enjoy reading. These readers do not change your manuscript, they provide overall feedback on the structure, flow, and readability of it.

Generally novelists use beta readers more than nonfiction writers, but both types of books can benefit from a reader's feedback. The following four steps can help you find and use beta readers:

1. Ask readers on your email list if they would be interested in being a beta reader. This person should fit into your target audience for the book. Also ask your social media followers and your writers' group members. Seeking input from friends is an option, but you would need to ensure that they would provide honest feedback without fear of damaging your relationship.

I invited an acquaintance who had recently become gluten sensitive to be a beta reader for my book *Solving the Gluten Puzzle: Discovering Gluten Sensitivity and Embracing the Gluten-Free Lifestyle*. Her insight helped make the book more reader friendly and not laden with medical terminology. Consider asking on Goodreads or in an online reading community. Usually three to five beta readers are sufficient.

2. Send your beta readers a polished manuscript—one that has been edited, because you don't want small grammar errors to impede their reading. Provide your readers with specific guidelines, such as a list of what you would like them to provide feedback on. This list could include your writing style, plot, story arc, character development,

dialogue versus description, pacing, and more. Some examples of beta reader guidelines include:

- Did you find the book difficult or easy to read?
- Did the narrative drag? If so, where?
- Did the book hold your attention from the beginning? If not, why?
- Where did the book get boring?
- What parts of the book could be cut out?
- Were any details repeated or redundant?

Also provide your beta readers with a deadline—anywhere from four to eight weeks. Follow up with your readers close to that deadline with a reminder that you are looking forward to their feedback.

3. Analyze the feedback and look for trends or patterns. If multiple readers agree on a specific issue, that is what you need to pay the most attention to. If only one reader is confused about a passage or problem, you may not need to address it. Read and reread the feedback and let it settle in your mind. Pray about it. Then decide which items you will implement and which ones to ignore. Incorporate the changes into your manuscript.

4. Thank the beta readers for their time to provide you with feedback. You could send them a gift or include them in the acknowledgment page in your book. I dedicated *Christian Study Guide for 7 Steps to Get Off Sugar and Carbohydrates* to my Bible study group, as the attendees were my beta readers. It would be a nice gesture to send each beta reader an autographed copy of your book after it is published.

Any book can benefit from a beta reader's review. Ask your

readers to write a book review you can use when launching your book and to be a part of your launch team.

Enhance Your Book with Endorsements

Securing endorsements is a crucial step in your book's prepublication phase. Ideally an author should start procuring endorsements at least six months before your book hits the shelves. If you are traditionally published, you may need to start this process twelve months before publication.

Endorsements from well-known personalities or famous figures can significantly boost your book's credibility and appeal. Initially, you might reach out to such individuals, hoping for a major endorsement that could skyrocket your book's visibility. My agent recommended I do this for my book *12 Ways to Age Gracefully*.

However, it's common to face challenges in securing such high-profile endorsements. I emailed about ten famous people (Joyce Meyer, Ben Carson, and the US Surgeon General Jerome Adams) whose endorsements would highly promote my book. None of them provided an endorsement.

Don't be discouraged if your initial attempts with famous personalities don't work out. Your profile is likely not high enough to get their attention, but it doesn't hurt to try. So shift your focus to influencers and professionals within your network who are familiar with your work and whose endorsement would still carry weight.

I compiled a list of forty potential endorsers I had a connection with, and I received over twenty endorsements. Think about former colleagues, industry contacts, or professionals who specialize in your book's subject. Since my book *12 Ways to Age Gracefully* was scientifically based, I asked physicians, chiropractors, and ophthalmologists I knew to write endorsements. Most of them did.

When someone agrees to endorse your book, send them an edited advance review copy of your book so they can read it thoroughly before writing their endorsement. I send a copy of my ebook (via

BookFunnel.com) because this platform sends a unique, nonsharable download link so only one person can open the document.

From the endorsements you gather, select the most impactful ones to feature prominently in your book. Typically, a couple of standout endorsements might find a place on the back cover, where they're most visible to potential readers. You can include other endorsements in the front matter of the book, providing prospective readers with insights on the value and relevance of your work.

My publisher placed two of the physician endorsements on the back cover and the rest in the front matter. You can also use blurbs from these endorsements in social media graphics. Prepare the graphics beforehand and start posting them when your book is released.

Keep in mind that platforms like Amazon usually don't allow individuals who endorse your book to write customer reviews due to conflict-of-interest policies. This ensures all reviews are unbiased and from readers not professionally connected to the book.

By strategically gathering and using endorsements, you enhance your book's marketability and provide readers with authoritative voices that validate your content. Remember, a well-endorsed book often stands out in a crowded market, appealing to readers who look for recommendations from sources they respect.

Create an Influencer Package

When preparing for your book's launch, engage influencers within your field by sending them a print copy of your book before its release. This strategy taps into the influencers' networks, potentially enlarging your book's reach before it even hits the shelves.

Make a list of influencers you know, and create a colorful letter, on superior paper, to send along with your book. I also wrap my book in tissue paper that corresponds with the book's branding colors. I've received books like this with the envelope color also matching the book.

The well-crafted letter should not only express your gratitude for their support but also outline actionable ways they could help promote your book. Suggestions can include sharing about the book on social media, mentioning it in newsletters, or simply spreading the word through their personal and professional networks. Here are some ideas of what to include in the letter:

- Encourage influencers to share photos or thoughts about your book on their platforms. They could create posts, stories, or even live sessions discussing why they recommend your book.
- Offer to write a guest post for their blog or to be interviewed on their podcast. These connections can engage their audiences in a deeper discussion about your book's themes.
- Suggest they host a book giveaway. Offering a free copy to their followers can generate excitement and increase visibility.
- Create a unique hashtag for your book launch and encourage influencers to use it. This can help track the conversation around your book and foster engagement.

You could even include a gift related to your book in this influencer package. Many authors have had candles, jewelry, or greeting cards created to match their brand. I've been the recipient of some of these gifts. Gift recipients are more likely to remember you and feel obliged to do something for you in return.

Influencers' approval can lead their followers to view your book as a worthy read, boosting pre-orders and sales upon release. Their reach and influence create a ripple effect that extends beyond your book's initial publication. When you engage influencers by sending them your book and provide a clear, easy pathway to support your launch, you improve the outcome of your outreach and boost your book's success.

Make a Book Trailer

Creating a book trailer is an effective way to capture the essence of your book visually and entice potential readers. Consider hiring a professional to produce a high-quality trailer, or you can do it yourself if you have the skills and software. The trailer should include engaging visuals such as video clips, images of the book cover, and graphics that represent the themes or scenes from your book.

Adding text overlays conveys the story's atmosphere and hooks viewers. Music also plays a crucial role. Choose a royalty-free soundtrack that enhances the mood and complements the visuals. Look for terms like "royalty-free" and "public domain" as these terms usually indicate that you can use the music without ongoing royalty payments.

The goal is to create a teaser that sparks interest and makes viewers eager to discover more about your book. I created video trailers in various ways to promote my books. For a simple approach, I used my iPhone to record a summary of my new book while sitting in my backyard. For a more professional touch, I hired experts to film a book trailer for my Healthy Living Series of three books. I took advantage of services offered at a conference where the recording occurred. I've also had a tech-savvy friend produce a trailer using music and graphics. You can view a couple of my trailers at Susan-UNeal.com/about-susan. With today's technology, you can find many opportunities available to produce engaging book trailers. I added mine to my website and post them on social media.

Update Your Online Presence with Your New Book

As your book's publication date approaches, update your online presence to reflect this milestone. Revise your profiles across various platforms to include your new release. Here's how you can ensure that your new book gets the visibility it deserves:

- Social media bios: Revise the biographical (bio) sections of all your social media accounts to include your new book. You could simply add a line about your latest publication or link directly to where it can be purchased.
- Author profiles on book platforms: Update your profile by adding the new book to your Amazon Author Central profile. On Goodreads adjust your author profile to include your latest publication and encourage readers to leave reviews. Ensure your BookBub profile lists your new book, taking advantage of this platform's ability to reach readers.
- Social media sites: On Facebook, X, and LinkedIn, post an update about your book launch and modify your profile to highlight your status with your new publication. On Pinterest, create new pins related to your book, such as cover images, quotes, or infographics about its themes. On Instagram and TikTok, use these platforms to post visually appealing content about your book, including video reels from interviews or book trailers.
- Your author website: Consider adding a dedicated page for your new book, featuring a synopsis, excerpts, endorsements, and purchase links. Explore influencer website book pages in your genre to generate ideas. If you already have an established book section, update it to feature your latest publication prominently.

If you fail to add your upcoming book to your Amazon Author Central account, your book won't be linked to your Amazon profile, and your Amazon followers will not be notified about your new release. By updating these platforms, you not only inform your existing followers about your new book but also enhance your discoverability to potential new readers. Each update helps solidify your online presence, making it easier for fans to engage with your new book and overall author brand.

Launch Your Book Team

Create a book review team several months before your book's release date. This team is vital for your book's promotion. I asked over 100 people to be on my team; seventy-five said yes. Here are some ideas for how to find potential team members:

- family and friends
- beta readers
- book club or writer group attendees
- fellow authors
- church directories
- Bible study attendees
- social media friends

Ask as many people as you can because about only half of your book launch team will post a review. If you want fifty reviews, you need a hundred people on your team. And don't let the thought of self-promotion stop you. Your book is about sharing God's message through your writing and making an impact on his kingdom. Your book is not about you, but about how you can help, entertain, or inspire others.

Weeks before publication, I sent a copy of my ebook (via Book-Funnel.com) to my book launch team members and asked them to please post a book review within the first week of the book's release. (For a discount on BookFunnel see appendix 1.)

When I published my book, I instructed my launch team to:

- buy the book the first day it is released.
- peruse 25 percent of the book on their Kindle app—

making them a verified Amazon reviewer. I told them the exact number of pages to read.
- write an Amazon book review during the first week of the book's release.
- post the book cover on their social media platforms.
- tell their friends about the book.

Ask as many people as possible to buy the book on a specific day so the book's Amazon rank skyrockets to number one, and your book gets that Amazon bestseller sticker. Assist your book launch team by sending them book promotion graphics for different social media channels. The more people you have posting on social media about your book, the better. (For information about a Book Launch Checklist, see appendix 1.)

I monitored which members of my book launch team had submitted Amazon reviews and which had not. At one, two, and three months post-release, I reached out via email to those who hadn't yet written a review, politely requesting them to do so. Persistent follow-up is crucial to ensure maximum participation.

As your book launch approaches, a well-organized team and strategic distribution of advance copies to team members is crucial. Actively engage your committed team to boost initial reviews and purchases and set the stage for a successful release. Remember, the effectiveness of your book launch reflects the effort put into these preparatory steps.

Follow up with your team to encourage their review submissions. Your attention to detail as you mobilize your support base can significantly enhance your book's visibility and sales potential, making all the preparation worthwhile. If attention to detail is not your strength, consider hiring a book launch expert if your budget allows.

Set Up Blogging Tours

A book-blogging tour serves as a valuable promotional tool for authors. This marketing strategy involves promoting a book across many websites through their blogs for a week or two. You typically pay the blogging business for these tours, but you could schedule several of your guest blogs to be posted over a short period.

For my book *12 Ways to Age Gracefully*, I negotiated with my publisher to fund one such tour. They strategically scheduled it to begin the day before the book's release, which proved instrumental in pushing the title to become a number-one Amazon New Release. In addition to the tour, I wrote about a half dozen guest blogs that were posted over three months, not one week.

This initial paid blogging tour generated about a dozen reviews on Amazon and Goodreads. While some bloggers provided honest feedback resulting in 2-, 3-, and 4-star ratings, these mixed reviews lent credibility to the 5-star ratings, demonstrating that the positive feedback wasn't solely from friends and family. This variety in reviews can actually enhance a book's appeal, showing potential readers a diverse audience has evaluated it.

Approximately six weeks postlaunch, I financed a second blog tour to rejuvenate sales as they declined. This effort yielded another dozen reviews and propelled the book back onto several Amazon bestseller lists. Such sales activity triggers Amazon's algorithm, prompting the platform to further promote books that perform well. Engaging in two paid blogging tours within the first six months of your book's release is a great goal, and so is writing and scheduling several guest blogs.

Determine Your Book Launch Budget

As you plan your book launch, it's essential to establish a budget upfront. Knowing how much you're willing to spend will guide your decisions on whether to complete certain tasks yourself or hire professionals. For example, your budget will affect whether you create your own book trailer or hire a professional, whether you coordinate the launch yourself or bring on a team leader, and how many paid blog tours you can engage in. Establishing a budget early helps you allocate resources efficiently and avoid overspending.

Seek Media Interviews

To prepare for your book's launch, query numerous media outlets requesting interviews. A great goal is to submit one magazine article and guest blog post per month, along with being interviewed on one podcast or radio show per month. Achieving or nearly achieving this goal can have a significant positive effect on your book sales.

Schedule these interviews within the first three months of your book's release and continue securing media appearances regularly thereafter. For optimal results, match the type of media outlet with your personality. (See further details on this strategy in chapter 10.)

Set Up a Book Launch Event

Throwing a book launch party is a great way to kick off your book's release. It's all about celebrating your hard work and getting the word out. Here's a simple guide to make it happen:

1. Choose a place that fits your book's vibe or where your friends and potential readers like to hang out. This could be your favorite cafe, a local library, or even online through a live stream if your friends are all over the place. For virtual launches, platforms like Zoom or Facebook Live offer a way to connect.
2. Set the date and time of the event when most of your friends are free to come hang out. Evenings or weekends usually work best for everyone. Make sure there's nothing big like a holiday that might keep people from showing up. Check for other large events in your local area to make sure they don't overlap.

3. For a live event, create a book banner that markets your book cover and title. For additional information on banners, see chapter 10 and appendix 1.
4. Make the event fun and engaging by having a question-and-answer session or bringing in someone else to chat about topics related to your book. Or you could conduct a small workshop, play games, or develop an interactive session.
5. Use your social media to promote the event. Make some cool graphics or a little video invitation. Don't forget to send emails.
6. Provide appropriate décor and food to make the venue inviting to your guests. When they are relaxed, engaged, and comfortable, they are more apt to give attention to your program and even purchase your book.
7. Pick out some parts of your book to read aloud and think about some answers to questions people might ask about your writing.
8. Make sure you've got plenty of books on hand for people to buy. Maybe throw in some fun extras like bookmarks or posters.
9. After the event, send a quick thank-you message to those who came. If they bought a book, ask them nicely to leave a review.

An author from my writer's group who wrote a book that included historical facts about her hometown organized her book launch event at the local library. The library had a slot on the local radio station, which they used to promote the event. She also spread the word to her friends and family in the area. The launch was a hit, with over a hundred books sold. A well-planned book launch event can significantly enhance your book's early sales and visibility.

Write a Press Release

A press release is an announcement to news media for letting the public know of something noteworthy. Your press release should highlight the newsworthiness of your book, perhaps by linking it to relevant statistics, facts, or trends that resonate with a broad audience. For example, I stated the Centers for Disease Control reported that 50 percent of Americans have a chronic disease and 42 percent are obese.

Grab the attention of the media with a headline that will entice them to read your release. Ensure the content of your press release emphasizes the benefits your book offers to readers—who are also their audience—explaining why it is a must-read. For guidance on writing a press release see appendix 1.

My local and regional newspapers have published several press releases about my published books and winning awards. One article heading read, "Local author publishes another award-winning health book." When a newspaper has a faith section, it can increase your chances of publication.

Print Promotional Material

Consider creating a book launch event card to share with family and friends. Design bookmarks that feature your book and website as well as business cards that include your book cover. Print these materials well before your book's release.

Utilize Amazon Advertising

Running Amazon ads is another critical strategy in book marketing. Amazon benefits from your book's success, so investing in their advertising system can significantly boost your book's visibility. Amazon ads can amplify your book's online presence by ensuring it appears before a targeted audience. Make sure you use your book's well-researched, high-ranking keywords in your ad.

The combination of a captivating cover, numerous Amazon reviews, and targeted advertising can increase sales potential dramatically.

I've found Amazon ads to be a vital part of my high book sale volume. I took a couple of courses to learn how to run Amazon ads. It took seven months to get the hang of it before my ads became profitable. But since then, for every hundred dollars I've spent on ads, I've made almost $200 in profit. Amazon wants their cut of your profits. If your book sells well and you split the profit, Amazon will display your ad before potential buyers, which results in more sales.

I negotiated with my publisher to pay for and run Amazon ads for the first three to six months postlaunch. A couple of weeks after releasing the book, the publisher activated these ads to ensure continued momentum in the book's visibility and sales. By sharing profits with Amazon through these ads, you can motivate the platform to further boost your book. Combine your own marketing strategies with the broad exposure offered by running Amazon ads to enhance your book's success.

In addition to running Amazon ads, publish guest blogs and magazine articles along with radio interviews to enhance Amazon's algorithm for your book. This multi-layered marketing approach not only drives immediate book sales but also builds a longer-term sales strategy.

Book Launch Marketing Timeline

This schedule helps you structure your launch preparations, making sure you finish key activities before your book is released. Adjust this timeline to meet your specific needs.

Six Months before Book Launch

- request endorsements
- submit your manuscript to trade publications for review (see chapter 8 for more information about editorial or trade reviews)
- find beta readers
- assemble your book launch team

Four Months before Book Launch

- produce a book trailer
- create social media graphics and a media kit (see chapter 10 to learn how to make a media kit)
- update your website, Goodreads, and social media profiles with your book's information
- arrange a book blogging tour (paid and on your own)
- seek media interviews (radio shows, podcasts, television, etc.)
- plan your book launch event

Two Months before Book Launch

- print promotional materials such as bookmarks, business cards, flyers, etc.
- mail print book to influencers
- write and submit magazine and guest blog articles related to your book's theme

Launch Month

- add your book to your Amazon Author Central profile
- distribute a press release announcing your book's launch to local and regional news outlets
- notify your email list about your book's release
- promote your book on social media

- publicize and send invitations for your book launch event
- conduct your book launch event
- ask your book launch team members to write an Amazon review
- create Amazon ads

By carefully planning and performing these steps, you will maximize your book's potential for success. However, you can't do everything. Choose the tasks that resonate with you most. What you don't accomplish with one book, you can perform for the next. I didn't create a book trailer until my third book. This career is like running a marathon, not a sprint. It takes time. Do what you can now and try new strategies later.

Summary

To launch your book successfully, you must prepare several months before the release date. Begin by enlisting beta readers to pinpoint and address any issues within your manuscript, enhancing the likelihood of receiving positive reviews. Secure endorsements from recognized experts to enhance the book's credibility. These endorsements may even be showcased on the book's front or back cover.

Implement a well-coordinated book launch team and distribute advanced review copies so you can generate early reviews. Follow up with your team members to ensure their active participation and maximize your launch efforts. By preparing early, engaging with potential promoters, and using digital marketing strategies, you can significantly boost your book's launch success.

Action Steps

1. Recruit three to five beta readers to provide feedback on your manuscript.
2. Seek endorsements from well-known figures or industry professionals to boost credibility.
3. Create and post social media graphics of endorsement blurbs when the book is launched.
4. Mail print copies of your book to influencers, along with a well-crafted letter suggesting ways they can help promote your book.
5. Produce a video book trailer to post on your website and social media platforms.
6. Update your online presence on all your author profiles and social media bios to include information about the new book.
7. Assemble a book launch team to help promote the book, provide reviews, and boost initial sales.
8. Schedule guest blogs and paid blogging tours to generate reviews and increase your book's visibility.
9. Write a press release and send it to local and regional media outlets.
10. Run Amazon ads to increase your book's visibility and sales.

Chapter 8

Ignite Book Sales with Reviews

Holding your published book for the first time sparks immense pride and relief. Congratulations, you did it! After grueling hours of writing, editing, and formatting, you can bask in the thrill that you birthed your divine-inspired vision. However, any seasoned author will advise that birthing the book was merely phase one. Similarly, once a child is born, for the next eighteen years you've got to raise him or her. The same goes for your new book. Now comes the feat of promoting your literary baby to ensure its success and longevity in a competitive marketplace.

One of the most critical post-publication strategies of book marketing is gaining a healthy number of positive reviews. These published reader perspectives serve as unpaid testimonials that will powerfully influence the purchasing decisions of potential readers browsing online retailers like Amazon.

When you get a substantial number of reviews, your book appears credible, popular, and desirable compared to competitors. Authentic reviews provide the social proof modern consumers seek before investing in an unfamiliar book. They substantiate your story's quality. This chapter will help you understand the importance of reviews and provide strategies to acquire them.

Pursue Editorial Reviews

There are two types of book reviews. You are most likely familiar with consumer reviews posted by readers on online retailers like Amazon. However, there is another powerful category—editorial or trade reviews from professional book review publications and organizations. Some well-known complimentary review sources include *Publishers Weekly* and *Library Journal*, though gaining their attention is extremely competitive. Many authors instead pursue paid professional reviews from reputable firms like Kirkus Reviews, BookLife Reviews, BlueInk Reviews, Readers Favorite, and Foreword Clarion Reviews.

Securing positive editorial reviews is a process that requires planning months before your book's publication date. You need the reviews early so you can post them during your book's release. Therefore, publishers and authors need to get ahead of the process by submitting review copies and materials well in advance to increase the chances of getting that sought-after editorial review. Some endorsements may carry enough influence to use on the book's cover or in the front matter. These trade reviews need to be received early enough to include them in the publishing process.

A glowing critique from any of these paid or free book-review publications, provides invaluable third-party validation. These reviews can be a game-changer for gaining credibility and interest from media and readers alike. While paid reviews involve an investment, they can increase your book's sales and recognition.

Boost Your Book's Amazon Credibility

In earlier chapters we've discussed the importance of hooking readers with an enticing book cover and description. Those polished elements create initial interest in your book. However, reviews may serve as the decisive factor to convert browsers into buyers. A positive review can convince buyers your book is worth their investment of money and time. When a book doesn't have any reviews, or very few, the reader's perception is that the book is not any good. Numerous convincing reviews provide the credibility to solidify those sought-after sales. A stunning cover may reel them in, but reviews bring them across the finish line.

Amazon reigns as the international king of booksellers. It sells a lion's market share with over 40 percent of print book and 70 percent of ebook sales. Consequently, Amazon is the place authors should focus their attention for collecting reviews. Ensuring your book has a robust number of Amazon reviews should be paramount to any additional marketing strategy. Stellar reviews on this platform are essential for successful sales.

An author needs to get fifty to one hundred Amazon reviews before reviews occur naturally. Amazon thought readers would logically write a review for a book, but I've found organic, unsolicited reviews are rare until you get over fifty of them.

It took me two years to get my first fifty Amazon reviews. Two years later, my number-one Amazon bestselling book, *7 Steps to Get Off Sugar and Carbohydrates*, had over a thousand reviews. Most of the reviews occurred organically without solicitation. However, the first fifty were the toughest to get. So if you don't have a substantial number yet, keep trying. We have to beg family and friends to purchase our book and write a review. Keep nagging them.

When I receive positive feedback from a reader, I graciously respond by thanking them and ask if they would please post an Amazon review. I always send them a *clean* Amazon link. If your Amazon link is not clean, it may contain a code that tells Amazon that you generated the link. If a reader uses this code to post a review, Amazon may not post it because it is linked to you.

My book *Christian Study Guide for 7 Steps to Get Off Sugar and*

Carbohydrates has over 200 reviews. Here is an example of that book's dirty link versus a clean link:

Dirty: www.amazon.com/Christian-Study-Guide-Steps-Carbohydrates-ebook/dp/B07G9SLNNW/ref=tmm_kin_swatch_0?_encoding=UTF8&dib_tag=se&dib=eyJ2IjoiMSJ9.l7ZIy6TU3K8kclkTUOl_NbUp-dFAZznHjEmR-hNlP_GjHjo71QN2oLucGBJIEps.UF5dtIrBTJAlozg38r8_im6iNuRE9kD_LRjY53m-Uuz4&qid=1718041636&sr=1-1

Clean: www.amazon.com/Christian-Study-Guide-Steps-Carbohydrates-ebook-dp-B07G9SLNNW/dp/B07G9SLNNW

To create a clean link for an ebook, remove all the coding from the link after the Amazon Standard Identification Number (ASIN), which is a code that uniquely identifies a product and ebooks on Amazon. You can find the ASIN on your ebook's Amazon page in the Product Details section. I create a Word document that contains the clean links for all my books. When I need a link, I retrieve it from that document, not Amazon. Send the same clean link to everyone when promoting your book.

It is vital to make it as easy as possible for readers to click a link and post a review. I also ask fans to post on their social media about my book.

Aim for ten reviews during the book's first week of publication. I ask for reviews when I give someone a book. Two months later, I follow up with a text or email asking the person to please post a review of my book by clicking on the (clean) Amazon link. I believe it is the least a reader can do when you give them a copy of your book. Solicit reviews until you get fifty—the magic number. If you would like more information about how to increase book reviews, please see appendix 1. Beyond just requesting reviews, actively encourage your supporters to generate social media posts and word-of-mouth about your new release.

Leverage Book Bloggers for Influential Reviews

In today's digital world, book bloggers wield a significant influence over reading audiences. Securing reviews from prominent bloggers in your genre exposes your book to vast new reader segments and generates invaluable buzz. The key is identifying and targeting the right bloggers to maximize your efforts.

Start by researching respected book review services and blog directories that curate listings of active book bloggers interested in providing honest reviews. Develop a targeted list of ten to twenty bloggers whose audiences align well with your book's subject. Craft personalized query letters expressing why their readers would appreciate your book and offer a complimentary review copy.

Some notable book review services and blogger directories to explore include:

- NetGalley.com: includes book reviewers, librarians, retailers, and bloggers. Expensive with no guarantee you will get reviews.
- BookReviewBuzz.com: affordable but is not Christian. It is for general market books.
- TheIndieView.com: includes a list of book review sites.
- BookReviewerYellowPages.com: provides a directory of book reviewer sites.

Don't simply blast a blogger with a generic query—take the time to familiarize yourself with each blogger's background, previous blog entries, posted review policies, and audience demographics. Establish a warm connection by commenting on their posts and engaging on social media first. This personal touch goes a long way toward getting on their radar for potential coverage.

Successful blogger outreach requires patience, persistence, and thoughtful pitches. But the payoff of positive reviews from influential book bloggers can be immense for driving book discoverability and connecting with readers where they gather online.

Use Book Giveaways to Garner More Reviews

A book giveaway provides exposure for your book and increases the likelihood that the recipient will write a review for your book. Host book giveaways on Goodreads, LibraryThing, and BookLikes. First, become a member and set up an author profile on the site. Next, host a book giveaway. Only give away one to two copies of your book at a time. Conduct one every few months. However, giveaways don't guarantee a review.

Establish Your Presence on Goodreads

Goodreads is a premier social networking site for book lovers, and over 90 million members engage on this platform. Therefore, establishing a presence on this site is a strategic move for any author aiming to enhance visibility and engage with a broader audience. Goodreads offers authors a platform where they can directly connect with readers. Interaction on this site can help you build a loyal following and increase your reader engagement.

When you create a free author profile on Goodreads, you can list all your published books, share updates about upcoming projects, and participate in discussions related to your genre or interests. Goodreads provides exceptional tools for authors to promote their books through giveaways, which can significantly boost your book's visibility. Authors can also gain insightful feedback from readers' reviews and ratings. In essence, Goodreads can be another element in an author's marketing strategy, helping grow your reader base.

Enhance Your Book's Visibility on BookBub

In today's crowded book market, gaining visibility and connecting with avid readers is one of an author's biggest challenges. That's why interaction on BookBub has become essential for both traditionally published and self-published authors alike.

BookBub is one of the largest book promotion services, boasting over 20 million subscribed readers. When you establish a profile on BookBub, you will enhance your promotional efforts and connect with a targeted audience of book lovers. Invest time in building your BookBub presence to expand your platform and connect with readers. First, claim your free author profile, which lists your bio, tagline, social media name, and books with buy links. Avid readers use BookBub to discover books matching their preferences.

Beyond the dynamic profile, BookBub offers paid book marketing services like featured deals, ads, and giveaway promotions to get your books in front of their massive audience. A BookBub promotion can increase book sales and rank. Be sure to have an optimized author profile for maximum influence from these promotions.

Seek Book Review Sites

You could also seek reviews on book review websites, both Christian and general audience. If you have a Christian book, stick with a Christian site so you do not get a negative review.

Some Christian book review sites include:

- Book Bargains and Previews
- Faithwebbin.net

General market review sites include:

- Readers Favorite
- Reader Views
- Feathered Quill Book Reviews

Receiving negative reviews is an inevitable part of being an author—even bestselling authors receive them. Don't let them affect you emotionally. However, persistent negative feedback might suggest that you need to improve your writing, perhaps by seeking professional editing or further developing your skills, especially if you're new to writing. These reviews can provide valuable insights that help you refine your work and grow as a writer.

As the CEO of the Christian Indie Publishing Association (CIPA) and Christian Authors Network, the number-one mistake I see authors make is not getting fifty Amazon book reviews. If your book has not achieved this goal, implement some tips listed above to get more reviews. If you would like more information on this topic, check out the course Tips for Getting More Book Reviews in appendix 1.

Summary

Even before your book officially releases, take key steps to build buzz, credibility, and those all-important early reviews. By consistently preparing and reaching out to others months in advance, you can build momentum even before your book is published. A healthy assortment of reader reviews and blogger endorsements signals legitimacy to potential readers.

Again, one of the most critical steps you can take to increase your book's potential sales is to obtain at least fifty Amazon reviews. After your creative writing marathon, you owe it to yourself and your book baby to give it every chance to thrive!

Action Steps

1. Send your edited and formatted book to editorial review sites months before its publication date.
2. Try to get ten book reviews during the book's formal launch week.
3. Ask for reviews when you give someone a book or receive positive feedback from a reader.

4. Continue to work on getting Amazon book reviews until you get fifty.
5. Send potential reviewers a clean Amazon book link.
6. Query book review bloggers to see if they would review your book on their blog.
7. Create an author profile on Goodreads and list all your books on this site.
8. Set up an author profile on BookBub. Investigate running a BookBub promotion.
9. Take the course Tips for Getting More Book Reviews on CIPA.Podia.com.
10. Request book reviews on book review sites.

Chapter 9

Amplify Book Visibility through Contests

Standing out in the crowded book world is no easy feat, but entering contests provides invaluable visibility that can launch your work to new heights. More than just bragging rights, strategic contest participation offers a multifaceted opportunity to gain recognition, bolster your author brand, and expand your audience. Winning book contests have helped elevate my books' status.

Imagine the credibility boost when you promote your book as an award-winning finalist or winner. That prestige becomes a platform to reach more readers. This chapter describes how to leverage contests to maximize exposure and take your book promotion to the next level.

Contests offer far more than just certificates and trophies to display on your shelf. They open doors for more reviews, book sales, and recognition. Success produces more success. Book contests should be a part of every author's marketing plan. Whether or not your book takes the top prize, the contest journey spotlights your work in front of enthusiastic new readers.

Dive into the world of contests with clear goals, organized record keeping, and persistence. Create a calendar and budget for entering book contests. Space out entries to capitalize on publicity opportunities. Mindful participation in contests, especially as part of a broader promotional plan, delivers compounded benefits that give your book wings.

Enter Book Contests

It may seem daunting to enter your writing in a competition against others who may write better or have more experience. However, even if you don't win, your name may be called during the ceremony or placed on promotional material. Name recognition is beneficial.

Entering and potentially winning contests should be a strategic part of your book marketing plan. Enter as many contests as you can the first year after your book's publication. Many contests are for only newly released books. After you have won several esteemed contests, you can stop entering them. I know an author whose book won ten contests. To highlight this accomplishment, she created a bookmark that includes her book cover, website, and all ten winner emblems. Now that's excellent marketing!

Finding reputable contests is the first step. Search online for book competitions, especially well-established awards sponsored by recognized organizations in your genre. Or find an association that provides a list of current contests. Longstanding contests with a solid history offer the most value. Many competitions are part of a major writers' conference. So check each conference you consider attending. The conferences with the most acclaimed reputation should move to the top of your list.

What are the qualities of a reputable contest? First check to see how the long the contest has existed. Is the contest associated with a conference? How large is the conference, and how long has it been around? Look for an award ceremony that applicants can attend, where winners are announced and receive trophies or plaques. (See appendix 1 for an extensive list of trustworthy contests.)

Vetting each contest is key. Thoroughly review the guidelines and entry requirements before submitting to ensure your book qualifies and you meet the eligibility rules. Many contestants unfortunately waste money by overlooking a critical detail that disqualifies them. Avoid this fate by carefully studying each competition and following instructions to the letter. Ask questions if the contest guidelines seem unclear. Many contestants are disqualified before their book is judged because they don't follow the instructions. Diligent prep work helps set your entry up for smooth sailing.

Some contests provide feedback for your writing. Getting an objective opinion of your work is well worth the entry fee. If the person who read and judged your book liked it, she may tell others about it or even promote it on social media. Some competitions donate the judged books to libraries or churches, circulating the books further.

Attend Award Ceremonies

Sitting among fellow finalists at an award ceremony brings a roller coaster of emotions no matter the outcome. The anticipation is tantalizing. During the opening remarks, stomachs churn with exhilaration before plunging into nervous nail-biting once nominations are read.

Hearing your name causes sheer euphoria. You feel emotions that can't be expressed in words. Legs go numb even as you must steady yourself to ascend the stage. Joy and disbelief surge in your mind as you accept the award. No words can encapsulate the significance of this milestone that culminates after years of diligent work. If you are a finalist, attend the award ceremony if possible.

Winning validates the countless hours spent writing every sentence, character, and plot twist. All the late nights tweaking scenes, rejection letters, and meticulous editing build to this pinnacle of public acclaim. No trophy or certificate can quantify the significance of such peer acknowledgment. Winning a book contest marks your induction into the upper echelon of this trade.

If you don't win, it is disappointing but formative. The only thing you lose is your entry fee. Defeat stings in the moment, but there's always next time. Being a finalist stands as evidence of your book's caliber. Tomorrow offers a new contest and opportunity to try again. With grace, objectivity, and persistence, an award becomes not the destination but merely a mile marker along your literary journey.

Honors from Book Awards

Winning respected contests sets your book apart, showing the reader that this book is superior. As an award-winning author, you gain the right to proudly display emblem seals announcing your achievement. Placing first, second, or third makes you a winner and typically entitles you to receive printable certificates and high-resolution artwork files of the contest seal. Strategically incorporate these into your book cover and marketing materials. One year, during the awards ceremony at the Blue Ridge Mountains Christian Writers Conference, I went up on stage twice to receive awards for the Selah and Directors Choice Awards for my children's book *Eat God's Food: A Kid's Guide to Healthy Eating*.

If you independently publish, you can add the emblem to your cover and upload it to the publishing platforms. Also add the winning announcement to the first line of your book's description on these platforms. The emblem and award-winning status usually result in more sales. If you are traditionally published, you can buy physical seals and attach them to the books you sell. The emblems visually showcase your book as extraordinary.

Readers equate awards with quality. That prestigious gold seal provides immense social proof, inducing readers to take a chance on your book over the masses of options. The emblem suggests superior writing, editing, and storytelling verified by industry experts. This credibility boosts book sales.

For example, after my book *7 Steps to Get Off Sugar and Carbohydrates* won the Selah award, I added the shiny gold seal to the cover, and for the next eight months, monthly sales quadrupled over my average. The social recognition of that respected Christian writing award propelled the book's ongoing interest. Winning contests can dramatically extend the book's profitability and lifespan.

Such achievements also open promotional opportunities through media coverage, features in industry publications, and the development of new relationships with retailers. The contest organization publicizes the winners and finalists through many media. This is free advertising. Having a prestigious award attached to your previous book can significantly boost your chances of securing high-profile endorsements for your next literary work, which often translates into increased sales and visibility.

After winning an award, distribute a press release about this achievement to local and regional newspapers and relevant magazines. If you need guidelines on crafting an effective press release, see appendix 1. Many newspapers will happily publish releases since awards elicit reader interest. Many papers have featured articles spotlighting my award wins, complete with photos of the honored book and award ceremony. Envision the expanded readership and potential new fans who will discover your book through this publicity. Combined with marketing, awards deliver a ripple effect that accelerates your book's success.

Leverage Award Prestige to Capture Industry Attention

Winning contests confirms you as a superior writer. In the competitive publishing world, contests offer a chance to prove your writing skills. Prestigious writing awards can capture the attention of literary agents and publishers because you stand out from the slush pile.

After a literary agent or publisher trudges through hundreds of queries and mediocre manuscripts, an award-winning unpublished submission can pique their interest. The recognition suggests your grasp of storytelling and polished execution stands above the rest. Experts vetted and validated your work.

Being an award-winning writer gives literary agents confidence they can sell your work and makes acquisition editors more eager to snag your manuscript before a competitor does. For example, winning third place at the Blue Ridge Mountains Christian Writers Conference contest for unpublished works sparked interest from an agent for my unpublished Bible study. Before the conference concluded, that prominent agent offered to represent me. The award recognition validated my writing talent.

Highlight contest nominations or wins in your query letters and book proposals to agents and publishers. List it on your one-sheet and website. Awards give you a step up in contract negotiations and advance offers as well. Don't be shy about listing awards in your author bio and email signature too. The validation helps you stand out from the pack.

Emphasize Book Awards in Marketing

Winning a respected book award unlocks a treasure of promotional opportunities. That laurel transforms your marketing from amateur to authoritative. Publicize the achievement everywhere and anywhere that displays your credentials.

An award increases the value of a book in the eyes of the reader. If a consumer is choosing between two books and one has a little gold emblem, the reader will most likely choose the award-winning book. Add the shiny seal on your book cover and put it on all promotional graphics. That visual cue sways browsing readers to take a chance on your book over the masses. It suggests elite-caliber writing recognized by experts.

Promote the win heavily on social media and in your emails or newsletter. This offers your readers an exciting reason to purchase your book. Consider taking out ads on Amazon and Facebook, in industry magazines, and with other media outlets, highlighting your award-winning status.

When contacting magazines, podcasts, bloggers, and television shows, include the information regarding your book's award. Pitch the news to local and regional radio shows in your press releases. Awards increase your authority and give media outlets another area to highlight in interviews. Media coverage expands your exposure.

Enter writing contests associated with the conferences you plan to attend. If you don't have a book, submit an article, devotion, or short story. Even finalist status brings marketing mileage whether or not you win. But that first prize elevates your credibility, not only as an author but as a speaker and workshop leader. My book *Healthy Living Journal* won the Golden Scrolls contest for Best Inspirational Gift Book. I use that tagline to advertise the book every Christmas season.

Summary

Entering writing contests requires finding legitimate book award contests, carefully vetting their guidelines, and maximizing promotion once a book wins an award. Winning respected awards provides invaluable visibility, credibility, and social proof that can significantly boost book sales and expand an author's reach. Even if you don't win, the exposure to a wider audience and expert critiques from judges will grow you as an author.

In our crowded market, winning an award, or even being a finalist, can open doors to a wider audience for your writing. Ultimately, you want to display award emblems and seals on book covers and marketing materials, which attract more readers. Savvy advertising cements the author's brand and sells more books. Media coverage and publicity through the award organization's promotions brings more recognition. Building an author's credentials and reputation can attract agents and publishers. Book contest participation should be an ongoing part of an author's marketing plan. Let your hard work and recognition unlock greater success!

Action Steps

1. Create a calendar and budget for entering book contests.
2. Research reputable book contests and strategize which ones to enter within the first year of your book's publication.
3. Carefully review all contest guidelines and eligibility rules before submitting entries to avoid disqualification.
4. When attending a writers' conference, enter an unpublished manuscript, published book, article, etc. into their contest.
5. If you are a finalist, attend the award ceremony if possible.
6. After winning, attach the award emblem to your self-published book. If your book is published traditionally, buy the cover stickers to display on your books.
7. Update your author bio, website, and email signature with your award-winning credentials.
8. Prepare marketing materials and promotional graphics incorporating any award wins or finalist placings to post on social media.
9. Advertise your award-winning status on platforms like Amazon, Facebook, magazines, etc.
10. Write a press release about your win and submit it to local and regional newspapers and radio.

Chapter 10

Steps for Book Marketing

Now that you have published and launched your book and begun collecting positive reviews to increase sales, the journey into marketing truly begins. A successful launch and new reviews only bump sales for a limited time. Consistent innovative marketing after your book is available to the public is the key to longevity in book sales.

It's tempting for many authors to jump into their next book once the previous one is published. After all, writing is the passion that birthed the desire to become an author in the first place. Yet the last thing you want is for your recent book to disappear before another one is ready to publish. So like it or not, you'll need to balance marketing and writing to keep your author career moving forward.

Before diving in to marketing, however, take the time to prepare and strategize for this essential phase in the life of your book. Start by assembling key marketing tools, such as a media kit and a visually appealing book banner. Then, evaluate which marketing approach best aligns with your personality to ensure a natural and effective promotional effort. Once prepared, you're ready to embark on marketing your book baby.

Assemble a Comprehensive Media Kit

Whether you're pitching to traditional media outlets or sending materials to bloggers, a professional media kit is crucial. This all-in-one document provides everything needed to promote and feature you and your book. Your media kit may include:

- book description, release details, genre, and key selling points
- book cover image
- author bio and headshot photo
- endorsements and excerpts of positive reviews
- sample interview questions
- links to your website and social media accounts
- awards
- contact information

An organized, visually pleasing media kit is invaluable for book marketing campaigns and demonstrates your professionalism. It is the easiest way to generate quality publicity. Create a media kit for each published book. If you have a book series, one kit for the series will suffice. Be sure to list all titles in the series, along with a brief description of each.

Well-prepared authors position themselves as true media partners. Besides a print-ready PDF version of your kit, create a dedicated page on your author website to host the media kit digitally. That way you have a sharable link to distribute the full package. If you snag an interview, the outlet will ask for your bio, headshot, book cover, and social media for promotion. Having this already prepared and in one place will save you time.

Anticipate media's needs by creating a list of potential interview questions for each book. After scheduling the interview, send this list along with the link to your website's media kit. Check out the Media Kit Guide, which reviews the ten essential ingredients to include in your media kit, at christianpublishers.net/free-gift. Do you need a graphic designer to create your media kit? See appendix 1 for additional author resources.

Create a Book Banner

In addition to a media kit, if you plan to promote your book at a launch party, book signing, or event, create a banner. Collaborate with a skilled graphic designer to develop a banner that not only captures the essence of your book but also draws attention from across a room. The design should be eye-catching, and the text must be legible from a distance, making it an effective promotional tool that enhances your event presence.

Consider this an investment in your book's marketing strategy. A well-designed banner can significantly boost visibility and attract potential readers at book signings and promotional events. See appendix 1 for assistance with creating a book banner.

Design Bookmarks

A superb way to promote your book or book series is with a bookmark. Include your website, book cover, and any other promotional information. My bookmark promotes my Healthy Living Series with three books on one side of the card and the megabook on the opposite side. It promotes four of my books on one bookmark.

Market to Match Your Personality

Consider your personality traits when choosing book marketing strategies. If you're an extrovert who loves interacting with people, activities like podcast or radio interviews, television appearances, or book signings will be more enjoyable and effective for you. If you prefer to stay out of the spotlight and enjoy writing alone, contributing to blogs and magazines may be more your style.

When you align your marketing efforts with your disposition, you're more likely to enjoy the process and excel in your promotional activities. I prefer being interviewed on a podcast or radio show rather than writing a guest blog or magazine article. It takes me less time to query and complete an interview than it does to write a well-crafted article.

Design a Monthly Plan

Create a marketing plan for each month following your book's release to maximize your book's sales. To receive a printable version of a book marketing plan for you to complete go to SusanUNeal.com/marketing. (See chapter 12 for additional information regarding completing your comprehensive book marketing plan.) Don't wait for marketing opportunities to come along; plan for them every year. Just like you raise a child until they become an adult, you should market your book until it is no longer in print.

A monthly marketing plan could include writing one guest blog, publishing one magazine article, and participating in a media interview, such as a podcast or radio show. You could also conduct an in-person book signing event. This goal is ambitious and might not always be achievable, especially when you are deep in the writing process of a new book. However, once your book is published, you must engage in these activities so readers can find and be inspired by your hard-earned work.

To stay organized and on top of marketing efforts, document and organize your plans and track your progress. Create a detailed tracking document listing each blog, magazine, and podcast you pitch to. This chart should include columns for the site or media name, host name, contact email, date of query, response received, and date of interview if applicable. Such a system not only keeps you organized but also saves you from the chaos of accidentally querying the same outlet twice—as I learned when I pitched to a hundred podcasters over eight months to secure thirty interviews. That year I won the Christian Authors Network Excellence in

Marketing Award, which affirmed the effectiveness of my marketing tactics.

Furthermore, charting your progress should provide an analysis of the impact of each promotional activity. After each media opportunity, evaluate how it affected your website traffic, Amazon book ranking, and overall book sales. This invaluable data will guide your future marketing decisions and help you understand which efforts yield the best returns and reach more of your audience. Check out information about the Marketing Tactic Worksheet in appendix 1. By continually assessing the effectiveness of your marketing strategies, you can refine your approach and ensure optimal outcomes. The results help determine which media to query in the future.

Launch with a Kickstarter Program

Using a Kickstarter program can be a strategic way for authors to fund and launch their books. Kickstarter is a crowdfunding platform where creators can present a project to the public and receive financial backing from a wide audience. I know an author who used Kickstarter as her book launch because she was an introvert and did not want to do interviews.

Here's how authors can use Kickstarter for their book launches:

1. Plan your campaign by defining goals for your Kickstarter promotion. Consider the total amount of funding you need to cover everything from printing and distribution to marketing and promotional activities. Set a realistic funding goal that reflects the actual costs involved in launching your book.

2. Create your Kickstarter page by including an exciting description of your book, your story as an author, and why you're passionate about this project. Include high-quality images of the book cover, sample pages, or even

teasers of the content. Videos can be effective, as you provide a personal touch to engage your potential backers.

3. Offer attractive rewards for different levels of pledges. Common rewards include digital or physical copies of the book, signed editions, exclusive access to additional content, or even the opportunity to be mentioned in the acknowledgments. Creative rewards such as bundles with previous works also entice higher contributions.

4. Actively promote your Kickstarter campaign through social media, your website, email newsletters, and other platforms. Engage your existing fan base, as these are your initial backers who can help drive momentum by sharing your campaign with others.

5. Throughout the campaign, keep your backers and potential supporters updated on the progress of the book project. Post updates about the campaign's milestones, any recent developments in the book's production, or behind-the-scenes content to keep the excitement alive.

6. Once your campaign is successfully funded, focus on fulfilling your promises. Deliver the rewards by the agreed timelines and continue to update your backers about the progress of the book's release and any follow-up events like book signings or readings.

Be aware, however, that using Kickstarter to fund a book project has its drawbacks. One significant negative aspect is the risk of not meeting the funding goal. Kickstarter operates on an all-or-nothing basis, so if a campaign doesn't reach its goal, no funds are collected, and no money is awarded to you. This can lead to wasted effort and resources spent on campaign marketing and development with no financial return. However, if you reach your goal, Kickstarter not only helps fund your project but also builds a community around your book before it's even released, creating a base of engaged readers who are invested in your success.

My author friend not only met her financial goals with a highly successful book launch but also won the Christian Authors Network Excellence in Marketing Award that same year. If you are satisfied with your book marketing efforts, enter your plan and results in this marketing award contest as they offer lucrative prizes and perform outstanding publicity for the winners (ChristianAuthorsNetwork.com/marketing-award).

Schedule a Bookstore Event

Bookstores present an excellent opportunity for authors to connect with new audiences and promote their work. Hosting author events can be mutually beneficial, as they draw in additional customers to the store while giving authors access to readers who might not be familiar with their books. If you're planning to use these events as part of your marketing strategy, you must approach them strategically.

To build a relationship with a local bookstore, start by becoming a regular customer. Purchase books that align with your book's genre, such as Christian living books, particularly in your area of interest and writing. Build a rapport with the bookstore owner and managers so they know you.

Before asking a bookstore to schedule an event, make sure your books are available through common retail channels like Ingram, as this makes it easier for stores to order copies. When proposing an event for the first time, a personal interaction is most effective. Visit the bookstore dressed professionally and bring along a selection of your books and a media kit.

I've found the holiday season, particularly from Black Friday through the first week of January, is the most optimal time for book events because of high customer traffic. I like to invite another author to join me to create more interest and draw a larger crowd. I promote the event on social media, and many bookstores do as well.

Once you have finished setting up in the bookstore, take some photos and share them on social media. I've had several fans spontaneously stop by a bookstore signing from viewing my Facebook post that same day. During the event, use eye-catching promotional materials such as banners, bookmarks, and a beautifully wrapped giveaway box. Ask people who pass by to drop their name and email into the box. Conducting a giveaway gets readers to your table to interact with you, and that might be all they need to get them interested in one of your books. You gain names to add to your email list too.

After the event, continue to nurture your relationship with the bookstore staff and management by sending a thank-you note or dropping by a treat. Your thoughtfulness can go a long way toward securing future collaborative opportunities. I've had stores contact me and ask me to participate when they were conducting a local author event. My efforts paid off.

Follow up via email with readers who entered the drawing. In addition to the winner's gift, you could send everyone a link to receive your lead magnet and direct them to your website. Bookstore events can enhance an author's visibility, provide an opportunity to connect with new readers, and build industry relationships that contribute to an author's long-term success. One step at a time.

Enhance Your Online Presence through Guest Blogging

A website's PageRank is a system used by search engines like Google to decide the placement of a webpage in an online search. A page that appears higher in the results gets more visitors.

One of the key factors that affects a page's rank is how many other websites link to it. Since 2005 Google has used a special scoring system that looks at both the number and quality of these links. High-quality links from well-respected sites tell search engines that your content is trustworthy and relevant.

For guest bloggers, this means it's beneficial to write for websites that are authoritative. When these websites link back to your site, the system boosts your page's rank in search results, making it more likely that people visit your site.

Therefore, guest blogging is a powerful tool to boost your site's visibility. By contributing content to other websites with high domain authority, you enhance your site's credibility and ranking. The higher your online home's ranking, the more likely your site will appear in the first or second page of an online search.

Domain authority is a scoring system developed by a company called Moz (moz.com) that predicts how well a website will rank on search engine result pages (SERPs). Search engines view websites with a higher domain authority as more trustworthy and influential, making them ideal platforms for guest blogs.

To identify sites with high domain authority, use tools like Moz's Domain Analysis at moz.com/domain-analysis. Look for domains with a score of at least fifteen. Domains with a score above twenty have moderate authority. Avoid sites with a domain authority below ten to prevent potential negative influences on your site's ranking. Guest blogging for a site with a domain authority above yours will improve your online home's rank.

My websites, SusanUNeal.com and ChristianPublishers.net, previously ranked under twenty, but after I hired a search engine optimization (SEO) analyst, they now rank over fifty. (See appendix 1 for information about Website Domain Authority Boost.) Both sites accept guest blogs, and if you're interested, you can inquire about submission guidelines at CIPA@ChristianPublishers.net. Each blog post on both websites includes visually appealing Pinterest pins that direct traffic to the blogs, enhancing both visibility and engagement.

Create a strategic plan for your guest blogging efforts. Aim to contribute to high-ranking sites regularly, as links back to your website will continuously improve its standing in search engine rankings. Include these potential guest blogs on your monthly marketing plan. Remember, each article you write should include a bio that points readers to your site, further increasing your website's traffic. By carefully selecting the right platforms and crafting quality content, guest blogging can increase readers for your site as well.

Expand Your Reach through Published Articles

Another avenue to market your book is to publish articles in online and print magazines. Begin by finding periodicals in resources like the *Christian Writer's Market Guide*. Research each magazine thoroughly to determine its target audience and the topics they publish. Review the subjects covered over the past year and choose a different topic that aligns with, but doesn't duplicate, the existing content.

Select an article topic that not only appeals to the magazine's audience but also ties back to themes in your book. This approach will hopefully pique the magazine readers' interest in your article and hopefully your book. Always include a link to your book and website in your author bio. This tactic funnels readers to your website and additional resources. In your query letter to magazine editors, highlight your qualifications and suggest a few article ideas matching the publication's editorial needs.

Pitching to magazine editors at writer conferences is an invaluable strategy. These events provide opportunities to meet directly with magazine editors and other influential faculty. Personal interactions can significantly enhance your chances of getting your article accepted. Face-to-face pitches often lead to successful publications because they allow you to establish a more personal connection and directly convey your passion and understanding of the topic.

I've always had success in getting an article published when I meet with an editor in person. Network also with conference faculty members who have experience writing for various magazines and can provide insider tips and contact details for editors. Learning from their experiences and following their advice will streamline the potential publication of your articles.

Getting your work and website published in magazines serves a dual purpose. Online publications enhance your visibility and credibility with search engines, improving your online authority. Meanwhile, print publications elevate your reputation among readers who value traditional media. Each piece you publish helps establish your professional reputation and expands your reach, benefiting both you and your audience.

By strategically using publications to share insights related to themes in your books, you not only reach a broader audience but also establish yourself as an authority in your field. This integrated approach to marketing through articles can significantly boost both your book's visibility and your professional profile.

Plan a Podcast and Radio Show Tour

Booking a podcast and radio media tour is a highly effective strategy for promoting your book. To market your book via this type of media, your first task is to find shows that align well with your book's subject. You can discover potential podcasts and radio shows through several avenues:

- Networking: Tap into your existing connections or ask peers if they host a show that aligns with your book's theme.
- Professional associations: If you belong to professional groups, check for a directory of members who are podcasters and radio media.
- Social media: Review the profiles of new contacts to see if they host a show. For example, I once connected with a doctor from England via Instagram's direct messaging. He hosted a podcast, and this led to an interview.

- Podcast matching: Consider subscribing to services that connect podcasters with guests, such as RadioGuestList.com, PodcastGuests.com, and PodMatch.com. These platforms can simplify finding shows that match your book's niche.
- Manual search: Although more time-consuming, you can manually search for podcasts on platforms like iTunes or Listen Notes. On iTunes, use the "You Might Also Like" feature on a podcast's page to discover similar content. On Listen Notes, you can directly search for podcasts by subject.

Before reaching out, listen to a few episodes to ensure the show's style and audience are a good fit for your message. When ready to pitch, tailor your approach by reviewing the show's content from the previous year. Don't pitch a topic the show recently discussed. In your concise email, propose three fresh topics that would interest their audience.

Address the host by name, compliment their show, and mention you wrote an iTunes review. An iTunes review for a podcaster is like a book review for an author. Briefly explain who you are, your book, and how an interview could benefit their listeners. Include a link to your online media kit or attach one to make it easy for the host to find more information about you.

Invest in a good quality microphone and ring light to ensure you look and sound professional, especially if the podcast also shares video content. During the interview, mention any promotional offers (lead magnets) you have. Make it easy for listeners to remember your gift by purchasing a domain name for it. For example, Saundra Dalton Smith uses RestQuiz.com.

After the interview, follow up with a thank-you email to the host. Once the episode has aired, continue building your relationship and enhance mutual promotion by connecting with them on social media. Share the podcast episode across your social media platforms and consider including it in your email newsletters to maximize exposure. By strategically using podcasts and radio shows, you can effectively reach wider audiences and drive interest in your book without significant financial investment.

Seek Television Media Interviews

Landing a television interview can significantly elevate your book's profile. You can get these highly sought-after interviews by hiring a publicist. This route can be quite expensive, but with experience and perseverance, you can learn to arrange these interviews on your own. It took me several years and numerous book releases before I figured it out.

Having a portfolio of several published books, particularly on topics that resonate well with current trends, enhances your appeal to television producers. For instance, my series of healthy living books tapped into the ongoing public interest in wellness, making them attractive for TV segments.

One effective strategy is to engage directly with the broadcasting community. You can do this through attending the National Religious Broadcasters Convention, which is the trade show for Christian media. Attending this annual event provides unparalleled media networking opportunities and can be a game-changer in your marketing efforts. (See appendix 1 about Trade Show Representation.) If you want to take your marketing to the next level, see chapter 12 where I cover how to get TV interviews by attending this event.

Enhance Book Marketing through Organization and Tracking

Effective organization and meticulous tracking are crucial for a successful book marketing campaign. To avoid the pitfall of redundantly querying the same media outlet, maintain a detailed log of all your marketing activities, in addition to your planning tools.

It's essential to assess the effectiveness of each marketing effort by monitoring your book sales, website views, and Amazon rankings during specific marketing periods. This data provides valuable insights into which strategies work. For instance, if a particular marketing approach correlates with a spike in sales or an improved Amazon rank, it's worth planning to use this strategy for future book launches. (Check out the Marketing Tactic Worksheet resource in appendix 1.)

To keep your marketing efforts organized, put together an annual digital document that lists all your promotional activities—guest blogs, magazine articles, and interviews. Include the media outlet title and links to each activity in the document. This way you can easily access these resources again if you need to review them or use them as references for future marketing campaigns. This method not only keeps things organized but also helps you maintain a collection of your media engagements, which can be useful for enhancing your professional reputation, as well as for highlighting your marketing experience in future book proposals. My annual document lists everything by month.

By maintaining detailed records and assessing the effect of your marketing strategies, you can refine your approach to book promotions, ensuring each campaign is more targeted and effective than the last.

Summary

Launching and marketing a book requires a multifaceted approach, combining both creative and strategic elements to ensure your work captures the attention it deserves. To effectively market your book, create a media kit. This all-encompassing promotional tool will demonstrate your professionalism to potential interviewers, bloggers, and media outlets.

For marketing, develop a plan that matches your personality and strengths. An introvert may prefer writing guest blogs and articles for reputable sites and magazines or use a Kickstarter program. Whereas an extrovert may enjoy a podcast/radio show tour or television interviews. Choose strategies you will be most comfortable with.

As an author you will have periods of book marketing and times when you will primarily write your next book. It's hard to do both at the same time. With my most successful book, I publicized it through publishing one guest blog, a magazine article, and a guest podcast interview per month. This strategy was sustainable for me as a full-time author. Continually adapt your tactics based on what has proven effective, and a realistic timeframe for your life and schedule, and always be prepared to seize new opportunities as they arise.

Action Steps

1. Check out the Media Kit Guide, which reviews the ten essential ingredients to include in your media kit, at christianpublishers.net/free-gift. Assemble a professional media kit for each book or book series.
2. Produce a dedicated page on your author website to host the media kit digitally.
3. Create promotional materials such as book banners and bookmarks to attract attention at events. Schedule a bookstore event during the Christmas holiday season.
4. Download a printable version of a book marketing plan for you to complete at SusanUNeal.com/marketing.
5. Create a marketing plan listing each blog, magazine, and podcast you aim to pitch to. Based upon your personality, decide what type of marketing best fits you.
6. Consider whether setting up a Kickstarter campaign for your book would be beneficial.
7. Write guest blogs and articles for reputable websites and magazines to enhance your authority and improve SEO.

8. Plan a podcast and radio show tour that aligns with your book's theme.
9. Pursue television interviews by hiring a publicist or attending the National Religious Broadcasters Convention.
10. Track marketing efforts to measure their effectiveness and organize their links on an annual Word document.

Chapter 11

Increase Your Income Beyond Book Sales

Making a full-time living as an author is a formidable goal. Most career authors do not subsist on book sales alone. Instead, they explore a range of strategies to diversify their income streams beyond books. Authors often find their earnings from book sales are modest.

Self-published authors typically earn between $3 and $5 per book, while traditionally published authors earn about $1 to $2 per book, unless they have a large readership and can negotiate better terms. Given these figures, book sales alone are not enough to sustain your ministry unless you sell a significant volume.

For instance, selling 1,000 books might yield around $3000, but advertising costs, such as running Amazon ads, could reduce your net earnings by an as much as 30–50 percent. As a result, it's crucial to explore additional revenue streams to support your ministry. In this chapter we will explore creating courses and digital products, pursuing coaching and speaking, developing an online summit (online conference) or membership, and becoming an editor.

Create Digital Products and Courses

Authors need to diversify their income streams beyond book sales. By using content they already created and crafting it into different formats, they can attract new segments of their audience who may prefer a more interactive or structured learning experience.

Digital products may range from a simple PDF to a more comprehensive e-learning module. Even a checklist can serve as a download. If you have material that is not enough for a full book, you can turn it into a product a customer can use. Authors often sell these products directly from their website, simplifying the sale process and allowing for greater control over pricing and profitability.

To drive traffic to your sales page, mention your product during radio and podcast interviews and include a link in your biography for magazine articles and guest blogs. For example, I offer the pamphlet How to Prevent, Improve, and Reverse Alzheimer's and Dementia (https://susanuneal.com/product/how-to-prevent-improve-and-reverse-alzheimers-and-dementia-pdf/) for $4.99 on my website, which earns more than a typical book sale. (For detailed guidance on how to create and sell digital products, refer to appendix 1.)

Creating a course is a fantastic way for authors to delve deeper into the themes of their books, whether you write nonfiction or fiction. For authors considering creating a course, identify topics that are in demand and you are passionate about. Successful courses typically solve a problem or fulfill a potential customer's need. The course value must be strong and straightforward.

For nonfiction authors, a course can expand on the concepts within your book, providing more comprehensive content and practical applications. Adding interactive elements and actionable steps within handouts enhances the learning experience.

Fiction writers can explore themes or elements within their stories, such as topics or thematic studies. For example, an author developed a course on how to overcome the dysfunctional relationships portrayed in her thriller novels.

I developed the course 7 Steps to Reclaim Your Health and

Optimal Weight to compliment my book *7 Steps to Get Off Sugar and Carbohydrates*. This course allowed me to enhance the discussion points from each chapter with additional material that wasn't included in the book. For each of the seven steps, I created concise videos, ranging from seven to twenty minutes, accompanied by downloadable handouts to provide further value. This approach not only enriched the learning experience but also significantly increased my revenue potential—earning $97 per course enrollment as opposed to around $3 per book sold.

When building a course, it's crucial to go beyond merely reiterating content from your book. Instead, focus on providing new insights, expanded content, and practical tools that can help participants apply the lessons in real-world settings. This added value encourages course sign-ups and can help support your overall author business.

Use a beta group to test a course before launch. This approach allows real users to check the content and structure of your course. Beta testers can provide insights and suggestions, ensuring that the course is polished before it reaches your target audience. I've been a beta user for a couple of courses and provided valuable feedback on ways to improve it. Engaging a beta group helps iron out kinks in your course.

You can host and sell your course directly from your website, giving your readers easy access to purchase and benefit from this extended content. Hosting a course on platforms can be expensive—there goes all your profits. So I found a WordPress plugin that allowed me to upload and host my course on my website.

Once a course is created, it can provide passive income over an extended period. You can sell it an unlimited number of times. Courses generally need minimal updates and maintenance, especially if the topic is evergreen—a topic that has consistent interest over time.

Authors who create courses elevate their status as an expert in their field. This positioning enhances their credibility, which helps them sell the course and their books, as they can often cross-promote these products. Developing courses may also open additional opportunities, such as speaking engagements.

Set Up Flash Sales

Creating a flash sale for your online course is a highly effective marketing strategy that can increase sales and boost your revenue. Put your course on sale once or twice a year. Email your list with 50 percent off in the subject line. Provide the discount for a limited time, like four days, which taps into an urgency that motivates potential customers to act quickly.

To implement this approach successfully, plan your flash sale around key times of the year when your target audience is most likely to make purchases. This could be during the holiday season, at the start of a new year, or even at the beginning of a school term. For my healthy living course, this would be in January. My sales usually increase right after Christmas.

Inform your email list about the upcoming sale and highlight the discount and limited-time offer in your email subject lines to grab their attention. During the sale, send a series of reminder emails. Start with an announcement that the sale is live, followed by reminders midway through, and a last chance email as the sale is about to end. Each one should clearly communicate the value of the course, what students will learn, and how it can help them achieve their goals. Also, share testimonials from previous students and include a strong call-to-action that directs potential buyers to your course's landing page.

Advance Your Expertise through Certifications

As an author looking to supplement your income, consider getting a certification in a field that aligns with your interests and background. For example, if you have a passion for counseling and wellness, explore certifications from the American Association of Christian Counselors, which offers a range of programs at aacc.net/. An author friend pursued a certification as a professional life coach and another specialized as a mental health coach. (See appendix 3: Certification Programs for more resources.)

I became certified as a Christian health and wellness coach, which was beneficial for me given my background as a registered nurse with a master's degree in health science. Initially, I charged $50 per hour for coaching, but as demand increased, I raised my rate to $100 per hour. In order to sustain our divine calling, we need to earn a sufficient income, as 1 Timothy 5:18 reminds us, "The worker deserves his wages" NIV. Without additional funds beyond book sales, it is difficult to support a ministry financially.

I also became certified through the Advanced Writers and Speakers Association (AWSA) as an author coach at awsa.com. Now I coach authors through the processes of genre selection, independent publishing, and effective marketing. Check out my coaching services at SusanUNeal.com. Besides the coaching certification, I received a speaker certification with AWSA.

Writing and speaking are distinct disciplines that tap into unique skill sets. Writing requires one to focus and engage with ideas over extended periods. It demands a mastery of structure, grammar, and style to effectively convey information on paper. In contrast, speaking relies more on immediate engagement, using vocal tone, pace, and body language to connect with an audience. Each discipline offers unique challenges and rewards, drawing on distinctive talents and capacities. My spiritual gift of teaching made obtaining a speaking certification especially beneficial, as it enhanced my teaching capabilities.

Here is some additional information about the POWER Speaker certification that AWSA offers. In just six weeks, students learn to craft powerful presentations, deliver outstanding messages, and master the art of storytelling that captivates. Graduates earn a prestigious certification that boosts their credibility. To learn more check out BePowerSpeaker.com.

Another excellent speaking program is Christian Speakers Boot Camp that was created and taught by international Christian speaker Robyn Dykstra. This eight-week certification launches aspiring speakers who graduate with a full-length, stage-ready signature talk. Check out this program at RobynDykstra.com/inspirational-speaker-training/.

After you become certified in a specific area, it's time to market. Create a webpage about the coaching you provide. I have a coaching tab with a dropdown menu for Author Coaching and Health and Wellness Coaching. Inform your email list that you are now certified in this area of expertise and provide the link to the page along with a flash sale on related products or coaching fees.

Launch Your Speaking Career

Speaking opportunities have a broad-reaching effect. After you've obtained your speaker certification, launch this new aspect of your career. Pursuing a calling in speaking as an author involves several steps to market and manage your engagements. Here's a guide to help you navigate the process:

1. Define your speaking topics: Identify the subjects you are passionate about and align them with your books' themes. List these topics on your website to give potential hosts a clear idea of what you offer.
2. Create a speaker video: Produce a five-to-ten-minute video clip of you speaking on one of your topics. Put this video on your website speaking page to show your speaking style and expertise.
3. Develop a speaking engagement assessment form: Prepare a form to collect essential details from potential hosts. This form should request information such as the

Increase Your Income Beyond Book Sales 153

organization's name, event dates, topics, the duration of the talk, the number of sessions, and the budget allocated for speakers. This information will help you evaluate whether an event aligns with your goals and requirements.

4. Set your speaker fee: Determine your fee for a typical 45- to-60-minute session. Fees can vary based on the type of organization (e.g., nonprofit or corporate) and your experience. Consider asking for a deposit of at least 20 percent upfront, with the rest due close to the event date.

5. Draft a speaker contract: Outline the items the event company will provide and the requirements expected from you. Essential items might include a lapel microphone, a clicker for your visual presentation, and provisions for your travel and accommodation. Make sure you understand any additional responsibilities the event organizer expects you to handle beyond the keynote speech. Speaking is exhausting, and you may prefer not to participate in any additional responsibilities after your speech.

6. Plan for products to sell: Make sure selling products is allowed at the event and part of your contract. Decide what you will offer at the event, such as books or course materials. Bundling a couple of items together can often lead to higher sales, especially if you offer something like buy two books and get a third one for free. One of the best ways to sell your books is at the end of a speaking event, and you usually unload a lot of them. After some events I've been so slammed I've found it best to have another person help me with sales. Consequently, I include in the speaker contract a request for event staff assistance with book sales.

7. Post event follow-up: After the event, send a thank-you note to the host and request feedback along with a

written letter of recommendation. You could provide your own feedback form for them to complete. Ask if you can share their comments with others. Also, ask if the event coordinator can refer you to other events or hosts who might be interested in your topics. Through this follow-up you can book new speaking opportunities.

8. Use online platforms and speakers bureaus: To find speaking opportunities, consider listing your services on platforms like WomenSpeakers.com, SpeakerMatch.com, GigSalad.com, and eSpeakers.com. These platforms vary in focus and can help connect you with both local and international events. A speakers' bureau can also represent you in finding engagements, but they require a commission, typically ranging from 20 to 25 percent of your fee. Some bureaus include PremierSpeakers.com, GoaSpeakers.com, and AmbassadorSpeakers.com.

By following these steps, you can establish a successful speaking career that not only enhances your visibility as an author but also provides a significant income stream.

Participate in a Summit

A summit is typically an online event that gathers experts within a specific field to share knowledge through focused sessions. Unlike writers' conferences, which offer a broad range of topics across multiple classes, a summit zeroes in on a particular theme, providing targeted insights and learning opportunities.

Summits offer an excellent platform for authors to extend their reach and share their expertise on a larger scale. There are two ways to be involved with summits: being a speaker or through organizing a summit and inviting other speakers to join. Either strategy can be a great way to reach new audiences.

A summit's lineup of speakers complements a chosen topic. For example, I've taken part in "Kick Sugar" and "Conquer Cravings" summits, subjects that correspond perfectly with my healthy living ministry.

Through the speaker's followers, a summit can draw a large audience. Most summits require speakers to have a minimum of 5,000 email subscribers and to send at least one, if not two, emails to them. This collaborative environment enhances the networking opportunities for everyone involved. It brings together a diverse group of experts, which can help you develop new professional relationships. Through these connections, opportunities for collaboration and cross-promotion may arise.

Summits offer an opportunity to generate revenue through ticket sales. A summit host can charge a registration fee upfront, but I've seen lots of talks offer free access and then charge for the recordings. This approach works well when you have a lot of excellent speakers and a short timeframe when the talks are free. Attendees often can't watch all the classes during the event, so they buy the recordings. Some events offer different tiers of access, such as basic or all-access passes.

An avenue to get additional funding is to solicit financial sponsorships from companies whose products or services align with the theme of the summit. In return for their financial support, their products or services are advertised during the summit or through other avenues such as website, social media, and newsletters.

Participating as a speaker at a summit provides a chance to present your work to a new audience who is interested in the topic and establishes you as an authority in your field. This speaking is effective if the summit's theme aligns closely with your expertise, like a healthy living summit does for me. It is an honor to be asked to be a speaker as it demonstrates your peers recognize and value you.

Search engine benefits arise from participating in a summit through links to your website and social media. Associating with other respected professionals in your industry can boost your credibility. Some summits include affiliate arrangements where you can earn a commission on sales. I've made more than $1,000 on a summit ticket sales affiliation.

I often join in healthy living summits, where the organizer invites me to speak for free. This exposure allows me to introduce my lead magnet and other resources—such as books, courses, and coaching—to new readers. These opportunities came more often after I improved my website's domain authority (see appendix 1, Website Domain Authority Boost) as I've become more discoverable online.

Overall, whether you're hosting or joining, summits can significantly boost your online presence, allowing you to share your passion, increase your audience, and grow your business in meaningful ways. To get started, look into existing summits within your niche or consider starting your own. Hosting or participating in a summit requires careful planning and execution, but the benefits for your career and professional growth can be substantial. I join as a speaker in several summits annually.

Build an Editing or Book Coaching Business

For those with a knack for grammar and detail, consider becoming a certified editor to supplement your income. Editors help others refine their manuscripts, articles, and academic papers. Many authors and writers require editorial services, from basic proofreading to more in-depth developmental editing. These services can offer a steady source of income.

Start by gaining a solid understanding of grammar, punctuation, and style guides—familiarity with the Chicago Manual of Style is valuable in the Christian publishing industry. The PEN Institute (PenInstitute.com) offers training for Christian editors through a variety of group courses and individual study programs to boost credibility and attract more clients. Editors who've been working for pay at least two years can apply to join the Christian Editor Connection (ChristianEditor.com), which matches authors and publishers with established Christian editors according to genre, editing specialties, and areas of expertise.

Begin with smaller projects or volunteer your services to gain experience and testimonials. If you are in a writer's group, offer free services as a way to start. Create a professional website showcasing your editing services, rates, and testimonials from satisfied clients. Marketing your services can also include attending writers' conferences and networking in writer and publisher associations.

By providing high-quality editing services, not only do you help improve the work of fellow writers but you also establish a stable income stream that can support your ministry while you continue to write and publish your own works. Several of my colleagues have successfully pursued editing careers, enhancing their income by providing editorial services to other writers. But remember, becoming a paid editor does not mean you won't need to hire an editor for your own writing.

Becoming a book coach can also be a fulfilling way to support your ministry and help others bring their writing dreams to life. As a book coach, your role extends beyond editing manuscripts. Instead, you guide aspiring authors through the process of planning, writing, and publishing their book. This support can be rewarding within a faith-based community where you're helping to spread inspirational messages.

Start by determining the specific areas where you can offer the most value. This might be nonfiction, memoirs, or faith-based children's books. Your background, knowledge, and passions should dictate your coaching niche. Create a structured program that outlines the journey you will take your clients on. This could include phases like concept development, outline creation, writing routines, and navigating the publishing process.

Offer personalized feedback, one-on-one sessions, and tailored advice to help authors find their voice and tell their story. Building a strong, trusting relationship is key to being an effective coach. I know it has been for me and my editor and book coach. She started out as an editor for a publishing company and, after editing hundreds of manuscripts in the nonfiction Christian genre, this experience naturally led to her becoming a book coach (see appendix 2 for her contact information). I would not be where I am today in my career without the help of my editor and coach.

By guiding Christian authors through the complex journey of writing and publishing, you're not just helping them achieve their publishing goals—you're also furthering your ministry's mission to spread impactful messages.

Format Interior Book Files or Design Book Covers or Trailers

Formatting and designing book interiors and covers are specialized skills that can significantly benefit authors. If you have a knack for technical details and design, you can consider offering these services, which can be a lucrative side business.

For interior book formatting, online formatting software like Vellum for Mac users and Atticus for PC users provides professional-grade layouts with ease. If you are tech-savvy and enjoy paying attention to detail, consider formatting books for other authors.

After paying hundreds of dollars to have each of my first three books formatted, I decided to format my own books. I enjoy paying attention to detail, so typesetting worked well for me. After purchasing Vellum, I paid for three hours of training from a coach. I saved a lot of money by formatting my next four self-published books.

Paying close attention to every page ensures the format is error free. Even after professional editing, it's crucial to review and proofread your formatted book rigorously. This process helps catch any lingering errors before publication.

When I upload my books onto the Kindle Direct Publishing (KDP) platform, before I push publish, I always send myself several proof copies of my book. I pay several proofreaders to read the book, and I read it myself, checking every page to ensure proper formatting. This process helps us catch most errors before the book is published.

After my proofreaders and I find the errors, I edit the formatted book in Vellum. With my first three books, I paid my formatter extra to make these additional revisions. Again, I saved money by learning to complete the edits myself.

If you are the creative type, designing book covers is another avenue where technically skilled authors can shine. Platforms like Fiverr, 99 Designs, and Upwork connect freelance designers with clients, and these platforms handle all aspects of promotion and payment processing. Make sure whoever you hire is familiar with the technical guidelines for covers on publishing platforms like KDP.

Someone on Fiverr created my Healthy Living Series of book covers. I found the cover designer through networking in Shelley Hitz's Christian Book Academy's Facebook group. Another author posted her book covers, and I loved them. So I asked her who made the covers. I contacted that designer and still use them to make my covers when I self-publish a book—like this one.

Learning to meet the KDP standards for book covers may require some effort and education, but mastering these skills can open up additional revenue streams. Whether you're formatting text or crafting covers, these skills offer the potential for significant financial returns.

If you possess video editing skills, consider offering book trailer creation services to fellow authors. An attractive book trailer is an essential promotional tool that can significantly enhance a book's visibility. Many authors, including myself, rely on these trailers to generate interest and excitement for both single titles and an entire series.

Creating a book trailer involves selecting fitting imagery, crafting engaging video content, and perhaps integrating voice-over or text to convey the book's theme. While I have paid professionals to produce most of my book trailers, I also took on the challenge of making one myself. You can view the one I made at SusanUNeal.com under book trailer. If you embark on this path, you'll be offering a valuable service that can help authors bring their stories to life visually.

Design a Membership or Association

Creating a membership site or association is an excellent way to use the many resources you've developed. This platform can offer exclusive content such as courses, guides, and other materials, providing value to your audience.

For example, an author who hosts a podcast wants to create a membership to support her audience of caregivers. She launched The Caretaker's Journey Podcast and website (TheCareTakersJourney.com), and plans to develop a membership that will meet the three major needs she experienced as a caregiver:

- encouragement through video and weekly devotions
- connection with others through weekly zoom meetings and a private Facebook group
- practical caregiver tips and tools shared through blog posts, book reviews, and a monthly newsletter

In 2004 Sarah Bolme created the Christian Indie Publishing Association to help independent authors navigate their careers. Two decades later, the association flourishes with over 500 members. A cooperative group founded Christian Authors Network in 2004 to assist traditionally published authors with book marketing.

Shelley Hitz founded Christian Book Academy (ChristianBookAcademy.com) to help authors write their books. Members receive access to a roadmap simplifying the writing process and streamlining the journey from the first draft to published work. The academy's supportive community helps writers overcome self-doubt and fosters a nurturing environment for spiritual and professional growth.

Do you have a membership idea percolating in your mind? Ask God to guide you. To create a membership, you need to select an online platform to house the resources. Here's how to begin this venture:

1. Identify what you can offer: Start by making a list of all the resources you have created that can be included in the membership. These could be video courses, downloadable guides, webinars, articles, and more. Consider how you can organize these resources into a coherent program that offers ongoing value.
2. Choose the right platform: Select an online platform that supports membership management and content distribution. Popular choices include Teachable, Kajabi, and Thinkific, which offer robust features for hosting courses, managing members, and processing payments. Platforms like MemberPress or Mighty Networks are excellent for creating more interactive community-driven sites. Podia, where Christian Authors Network (CAN) and Christian Indie Publishing Association (CIPA) are housed, is an excellent membership platform.
3. Structure your membership levels: Decide if you will offer different membership levels. For example, you might have a basic level offering access to articles and newsletters, and a premium level that includes live webinars and group coaching sessions. Each level should offer progressively greater value.
4. Set membership fees: Determine how much members will pay to access your resources. Consider offering monthly and annual payment options. Pricing should reflect the value provided and compete with similar offerings in your market. I've chosen to provide an annual payment plan for CAN and CIPA since I wouldn't want someone to gain access to all the material and unsubscribe the next month.
5. Develop exclusive content: Regularly create content that is exclusive to your members. This information could be anything, such as live webinars, early access to new materials, or member-only question-and-answer sessions.

The key is to make the membership feel valuable. I provide a twenty-page digital newsletter with industry news, book marketing tips, and promotion of members' new releases for CAN and CIPA members.

6. Marketing and promotion: Use your existing channels to promote your membership site—your social media profiles, newsletters, and collaboration with other authors or marketers. Highlight your successes, such as client testimonials, on your website and in promotional materials. Consider offering a trial period or a discount for the first month to attract new members.

By building a membership site, you not only create a steady revenue stream but also strengthen your relationships with your audience by providing them with consistent, high-value content that supports their needs.

Determine Book Categories and Keywords or Create Amazon Ads for Authors

Another way to support your ministry is through providing two highly technical aspects of book publishing—determining book categories and keywords through using the software Publisher Rocket. (See appendix 1 to learn how to receive 30 percent off Publisher Rocket.) Amazon uses categories to rank books. Selecting the right Amazon categories and keywords for your book is crucial for boosting its visibility and sales. Amazon categorizes books to help readers find them, and these categories can be highly competitive. The more competition a category has, the harder it is for a book to attain a high rank and vice versa.

Typically, an author or publisher places a book in three Amazon categories on the KDP platform. An author or publisher needs to strategically select categories with less competition to boost the book's ranking. For instance, when I reclassified my book *7 Steps to Get Off*

Sugar and Carbohydrates from the broad "diet" category to the more specific "healthy diet" category, it soared to number one, illustrating how a strategic choice can lead to bestseller status. All it took was this one change, and the book became a number-one Amazon bestseller.

For my traditionally published books, I've asked the publisher if they would like me to determine the categories and keywords. Two different publishers agreed. I spent half a day researching the most strategic choices. The publisher's staff may not have that much time to devote to this task.

Keywords are another critical factor in optimizing your book's discoverability. Amazon allows you to list seven keywords for each ebook and print book. That's fourteen keywords, not just seven. Amazon needs more information about your book to get it into the readers' hands.

It's essential to select keywords that not only define your book but also have a high search volume on Amazon. For example, the keywords I selected for *Solving the Gluten Puzzle* generate over 18,000 searches every month. Choose and update these keywords in your book's details on platforms like Kindle Direct Publishing, IngramSpark, or Lightning Source.

Due to the vast number of potential Amazon categories (over 12,000 for ebooks and print books) and millions of potential keywords, figuring out the best ones for your book can be a daunting task. Therefore, I provide the service to help authors determine the most effective categories and keywords for their books, and you could too. You can find more details about this service at SusanUNeal.com.

Amazon ads are an effective strategy to increase your book sales by ensuring your book appears at the top of results on their site when potential buyers search for similar topics. When someone researches a book to purchase, seeing your book first can directly lead to a sale.

I have had exceptional success with Amazon ads. I created my first ad in 2017, but it took seven months of monitoring the ads to figure out the system to make a profit. However, the effort was worthwhile. For every hundred dollars I spent, I earned nearly two hundred, doubling my investment. The process involves monitoring and adjusting the ads to maximize their effectiveness, which can be overwhelming but is a critical skill for successful book marketing. To learn how to create Amazon ads see appendix 1.

Once you've mastered this advertising system, you could provide ad management services to other authors. This not only helps them boost their visibility and sales but also provides you with an additional income stream. Learning and using Amazon ads can be a powerful tool in any author's marketing arsenal.

Summary

We all need to support our businesses financially. There are various ways you can boost your income as an author, aside from selling books. You've learned about the development of digital products and online courses, which can tap into different ways readers consume content. The chapter also discussed the benefits of obtaining professional certifications and engaging in coaching to add to your expertise and revenue. It guided you on launching a speaking career and organizing or participating in summits, which are powerful platforms for reaching new audiences.

For those with a knack for detail, you might venture into editing, as well as book formatting and cover design. Creating a membership site or association to build a community around your content can be profitable. Finally, you might gain insights on strategically choosing book categories and keywords for Amazon, as well as setting up effective Amazon ads, for other authors. These ideas will help you find the right mix of activities that fit your skills to grow your income.

Do you have an idea you've thought about pursuing? First, ask God for clarification if you should develop that idea further. Investigate certifications, coaching programs, courses, or any other avenue to acquire more knowledge. Gain the education needed and fulfill that God-given dream.

Action Steps

1. Develop digital products like books or checklists related to your book's subject to sell on your website.
2. Design courses that delve deeper into your book's content to engage and educate your audience.
3. Enhance your credibility by becoming certified in areas connected to your writing so you can offer professional services.
4. Start a speaking career to share your insights and sell books directly to attendees.
5. Organize or participate in online summits to gain exposure, network with other experts, and promote your products.
6. Become a book coach or editor to help others write their books.
7. Format books for authors using software like Vellum or Atticus.
8. Design book covers or book trailers for other authors.
9. Create a membership site where members can access exclusive content for a recurring fee.
10. Learn how to determine book categories and keywords for Amazon's advertising for other authors.

Chapter 12

Expand Your Reach through Advanced Marketing Strategies

In today's interconnected world, authors have multiple ways to share their message and build their platform. This chapter explores advanced strategies to expand your book's reach. These methods go beyond the conventional approaches to market your book and boost sales. We will explore the effectiveness of trade shows such as the National Religious Broadcasters Convention, Christian Product Expo, homeschool conventions, and denominational conventions to get your book in front of more readers.

If you're a children's author, you could also offer school visits. Maybe you would like to start a podcast or a YouTube channel. These techniques go beyond what a typical author does for book marketing. These methods when combined strategically can significantly boost your sales.

What it takes to sell 1,000 books in a month is a strategic, multi-layered marketing plan. The latter section of this chapter provides a step-by-step guide to develop a comprehensive marketing plan that can help you achieve that milestone.

Attend the National Religious Broadcasters Convention

The National Religious Broadcasters (NRB) Convention is a premier event for Christian communicators, attracting a global audience of media and ministry professionals. Attending this convention provides an unmatched opportunity to network directly with Christian radio, podcast, and television outlets. Basically, you can get a year's worth of media interviews through this strategic venue. For example, one year I secured five television interviews from connections made at the NRB Convention.

Be sure to attend NRB with a booth because that is the only way you can get the list of media attending the trade show. You can attend NRB with the Christian Indie Publishing Association (CIPA) and Christian Authors Network (CAN) booth. (For detailed information on how to attend with CAN and CIPA, refer to appendix 1 or check out ChristianPublishers.net/trade-shows/).

Before the show, contact the media that is relevant to your brand to set up interviews. While most interviews happen during the convention, some may be scheduled for later dates. In my experience, I've continued to receive inquiries from television stations months after just dropping off my media kit at their NRB booths. Some members have successfully scheduled a dozen media engagements, including appearances on television shows.

Participate in the Christian Product Expo

The Christian Product Expo (CPE) (cpeshow.com) is an essential trade show for authors aiming to have their books carried in Christian retail stores. Attending this event, which typically sees participation from over a hundred retail stores, offers a unique opportunity to connect directly with retailers. To maximize your exposure and increase the chances of getting your book into stores, attend with a booth such as CIPA and CAN, so retailers can buy your book. This would improve the likelihood that retailers, many of whom own multiple stores, will purchase and stock your title.

For members of CAN and CIPA, there are affordable options to gain exposure for your books among independent Christian retailers even if you cannot attend in person. Alternatively, you can attend the expo, which provides a fantastic platform to showcase your books to retail buyers. The show takes place annually in August, when retail stores are stocking up for the Christmas season.

One highlight of the CPE is the bookstore/author event held on the first evening of the conference. Participating allows you to have your book cover and headshot featured in the CPE program. During the event, up to a hundred bookstore owners visit your table to receive a signed copy of your book, increasing the likelihood that they will choose to stock your book in their stores. This event allows you to engage directly with retailers who can help expand your book's reach.

Display Your Books at Denominational Conventions

Attending denominational conventions offers Christian authors a platform to promote their books directly to church leaders and communities. These conventions gather members from specific denominations, presenting an opportunity for authors to connect with a targeted audience that shares specific religious beliefs and values. This approach can be more effective than broader Christian events because the attendees share the denominational themes and teachings that might appear in your books.

By setting up a booth at these conventions, authors can showcase their books and directly engage with pastors, church leaders, and laypersons who are often looking for new resources. Conventions often feature dedicated times for authors to present talks, which can further highlight your expertise and the value of your books to potential buyers.

These events are typically annual or biannual, which means they can become a regular part of an author's marketing strategy. This ongoing presence can lead to word-of-mouth promotion within the church community, significantly extending the reach of your book promotions. Authors may also gain insights into the specific needs and interests of church communities, allowing them to tailor future writings to better serve and resonate with this audience.

A CIPA member (CecilTaylorMinistries.com) who writes Bible studies sets up a booth each year at the regional United Methodist Church annual conference. He finds this strategy effective not only for immediate sales during the event but also for securing repeat business afterward. To maximize his visibility, he uses a slide show, displays a banner, distributes promotional pens, and provides his media kit. He sells his books directly at the conference, often covering the cost of the booth. This approach has sparked many meaningful conversations, significantly boosting his brand recognition among the churches that attend the event.

Set Up a Booth at Homeschool Conventions

Homeschooling has seen significant growth, especially following the pandemic. There are many homeschool mail-order catalogs and online bookstores, each with its own criteria for selecting educational materials. These platforms offer avenues for promoting your books through advertising or contributing educational articles.

Across the country, hundreds of homeschool conventions take place each year. By conducting an online search, you can easily locate a convention near you where you can exhibit. Setting up a booth at these conventions allows you to display and sell your materials directly to interested educators and parents.

Authors can collaborate to share booth space, which reduces costs and provides a larger selection of books. As the homeschool market continues to expand, the demand for diverse educational content increases, presenting a valuable opportunity for authors. Homeschool conventions are a gateway for authors and publishers aiming to tap into the homeschooling market.

No matter which type of convention you choose to attend,

remember to budget and schedule for items needed as a booth participant or vendor for your own booth: registration fees; marketing materials such as banners, bookmarks, your media kit, etc.; travel and accommodation expenses; copies of your book for signings and giveaways.

Schedule School Visits

Your role as a children's author opens doors to inspiring students through school presentations, whether in-person or virtual. Children are naturally fascinated by authors and the stories behind their books. When choosing schools to visit, consider your content. Secular books are best suited for public schools, while books with Christian themes align well with Christian schools.

Begin by developing several presentation options and put them on your website. Start with modest pricing and gradually increase your rates as demand grows. Make it easy for schools to book you by including an online application form with integrated payment options. Adding a video clip of your presentations helps schools see your speaking style and engagement with students.

To market your school visits, design a colorful postcard and mail it to school librarians within a reasonable driving distance. The postcards, combined with your professional website featuring sample videos, will help schools understand the value you'll bring to their students.

After you schedule your visit, tell the school what you need, such as a projector, chalkboard, or flip chart with markers. Send the school handouts for participating students and a book order form to have families complete along with payment before the day of your visit. To create a more personal connection, ask teachers to have their students write questions for you. You could ask for these questions before your presentation to create an interactive experience.

Professional children's authors often charge substantial fees for their presentations. For instance, author Taryn Souders charges more than $1,000 for a full-day presentation, demonstrating the value schools place on author visits. Check out her website at TarynSouders.com.

Start a Podcast or YouTube Show

Another way to market your book and broaden your platform is to host a podcast or YouTube channel. A show can help you gain a whole new readership. Your ministry is about serving others—focusing on what your audience needs and how you can meet those needs. You can serve them well by providing information during a show. Pray and ask God whether you should pursue one of these endeavors.

Starting a show begins with understanding your purpose and target audience. Clearly define your "why" (the purpose for starting your show) and your "who" (the specific audience you'll serve). Preparation helps ensure your message reaches the right listeners and allows you to address their unique needs, questions, and pain points.

There is a lot to learn about becoming a host. First you need to gain knowledge. The technical process of launching either a podcast or YouTube channel involves five key steps:

1. naming and branding your show
2. deciding on a format (solo or interview-based)
3. recording and editing content
4. publishing your work
5. promoting your show across various platforms

Your show's name should be unique, and your format should align with both your strengths as a host and your audience's needs. When using editing software, focus on serving your audience rather than achieving perfection.

As you launch, start with a bank of three episodes to give listeners or viewers enough initial content to engage with. Your show should have professional-quality audio, captivating cover art, and music to attract and retain listeners. Promotion is crucial—use your website and social media channels where your target audience is active and encourage listeners and guests to subscribe and leave reviews to help grow your audience.

Before uploading your content, it's essential to research your competition, explore trending topics within your niche, and conduct keyword research to understand what potential viewers are searching for. This preparation ensures your content not only resonates with your audience but also has the potential to be discovered through search engines or YouTube's search algorithm.

Creating quality content may require some investment in equipment based on your specific needs. Starting with a smartphone is perfectly acceptable for many creators, but ultimately you need additional gear such as an external microphone, lighting equipment, or a tripod to enhance production quality. The key is to focus first on creating valuable content consistently, rather than getting caught up in having perfect equipment from the start.

Content creators on both YouTube and podcasting platforms have multiple avenues for monetization. The most straightforward method is through advertising revenue: YouTube creators can join the YouTube Partner Program once they reach 1,000 subscribers and 4,000 watch hours, while podcasters can incorporate sponsored ads. You can diversify your income through crowdfunding platforms like Patreon and affiliate marketing where you earn commissions from recommended products.

You can also promote your own related products such as online courses, coaching services, or digital products. The key to successful monetization lies in building a loyal audience first and then strategically implementing these various revenue streams without compromising the quality or authenticity of the content that attracted viewers or listeners in the first place. Starting a show offers creators the opportunity to share their passion with a global audience while potentially building a sustainable income stream.

Create a Marketing Plan

To be an award-winning, bestselling author you need a multifaceted approach to book marketing. No one specific technique causes a book to sell well. In this book we have reviewed many strategies as successful marketing takes a snowball effect. I used layers of techniques to get one of my book's overall Amazon ranking to 4,400, which is better than 99 percent of Amazon's books.

To achieve that ranking, I attended the National Religious Broadcasters (NRB) convention where I met a television representative from Atlanta. Of course, I pitched my books and dropped off my media kit. From this marketing effort, I landed four interviews where we discussed five of my books. I highly recommend attending NRB.

They recorded my first television interview over Zoom. After that, I asked if I could drive to their studio for an additional interview. The studio scheduled three interviews with me. One show was broadcast live on television. These three shows aired over three months, which gave my book repeated exposure.

Also, a month prior to my book's best Amazon rank, I appeared on the cover of *Leading Hearts* magazine, which included a feature article about me becoming the director of the Christian Authors Network and Christian Indie Publishing Association. The day after my fourth television show ran, my book's ranking jumped to 4,400, and I sold well over 1,000 books that month. Consumers often need to see the product several times before making a purchase.

Remember, the level of marketing you choose will vary based on your time, work situation, budget, and goals. In any case, you will need to employ a variety of marketing strategies that can build on each other to find the readers for your ministry's message. Don't let the amount of information here stop you or intimidate you. Start where you can and commit to move forward from there.

Now let's develop your multifaceted approach through completing your marketing plan. Fill in your plan after reviewing each chapter's action steps, which are listed at the end of this chapter. Use these steps as a guide to create your comprehensive marketing strategy. Receive a printable version of this twelve-month marketing plan at SusanUNeal.com/marketing or Sell1000BooksAMonth.com.

Twelve-Month Marketing Plan

Month 1_____: Setting the Foundation

- **Course to Enhance Skills**:
    - *I will take the following course:*

    _____
    _____

- **Knowledge Expansion**:
    - *I will read the following guide, book, or newsletter:*

    _____
    _____

- **Strategic Investment**:
    - *I will invest in the following product:*

    _____
    _____

- **Marketing Focus Areas**:
    - *Primary marketing goal for this month:*

    _____
    _____

- *Key marketing tactics I will use:*

- *How I will measure success:*

  _____
  _____

- **Monthly Reflection:**
  - *What worked well this month:*

  _____
  _____

- *Challenges faced:*

  _____
  _____

- *Spiritual insight or quote*

  _____
  _____

Review Each Chapter's Action Steps

Review the action steps summarized below and use them to complete your marketing plan.

Chapter 1 Action Steps

1. Determine if your writing style is a plotter or a pantser.

2. Figure out the best time of day for you to write, and schedule writing into your calendar.
3. Create your book's outline.
4. Write without editing.
5. Join a Christian writers' group in your area or online.
6. Read writing-craft books to improve your prose.
7. Use a paid version of an online editor to edit your work.
8. Decide whether to use beta readers, and if so, identify them.
9. Edit your manuscript.
10. Find a developmental editor to edit your manuscript.

Chapter 2 Action Steps

1. Pray and reflect on the divine purpose behind your writing to identify your divine calling.
2. Establish a clear vision statement for your writing career.
3. Write a mission statement explaining the purpose of your writing ministry.
4. Create a document outlining your business's vision, mission, goals, and strategies.
5. Perform annual planning and schedule quarterly reviews of your plan.
6. Consider hiring support, such as a virtual assistant, graphic designer, or webmaster, to handle aspects of your business that are outside of your expertise.
7. Identify your intrinsic values and ensure your brand and promotional materials reflect your values.
8. Determine your target audience and how you can help them through your writing ministry.
9. Get a professional headshot to use with your branding.
10. Develop your brand, including a branding sheet.

Chapter 3 Action Steps

1. Buy at least one domain name for your website.
2. Schedule a photo shoot in your home, garden, or other setting relevant to your work. Use the photos in your website.
3. Develop a professional author website.
4. Create a lead magnet and its landing page. Monitor how often the lead magnet is being downloaded to gain email subscribers.
5. Buy a memorable domain name for your lead magnet to share during interviews.
6. Select an email marketing service provider to manage your subscriber list.
7. Connect your lead magnet's landing page to your email marketing provider.
8. Write an automated welcome email sequence (two to three emails in one week).
9. Produce either a newsletter or automated email sequence sent every seven to ten days.
10. Add affiliate offers to your emails to generate additional income.

Chapter 4 Action Steps

1. Review different writer conferences and register for one that fits your needs.
2. Create a business card to share at the conference with other attendees.
3. Schedule to get a headshot if you don't have one yet.
4. Make a comprehensive preconference plan.
5. Create a one-sheet and possibly a book proposal to give to publishers or agents at a conference.
6. Figure out your best writing genre and stick to it.
7. Read writing-craft books to improve your prose.
8. Read books in the genre you write in.

9. Build your social media platform by friending other authors.
10. Choose two social media sites that you will primarily focus on.

Chapter 5 Action Steps

1. Blog to drive traffic to your website.
2. Learn about the SEO techniques to use in your blogs.
3. Take the course Blogging to Drive Traffic to Your Website at CIPA.Podia.com.
4. Purchase the software program Publisher Rocket to help you identify the best keywords for your blog and book as well as your book's best Amazon categories.
5. Define your website's keywords you want to rank for on search engines.
6. Sprinkle those keywords into your blogs and blog titles.
7. Add Pinterest pins to each blog and pin them on your Pinterest boards.
8. Determine your book's keywords and incorporate them into your book's title, subtitle, and description.
9. Identify your books categories with less competition where your book can rise in Amazon ranking.
10. Take the course Improve Your Book's Amazon Rank through Expanding Categories and Strengthening Keywords at CIPA.Podia.com.

Chapter 6 Action Steps

1. When negotiating a traditionally published book contract, have a literary agent represent you. Negotiate additional terms to boost your books visibility.
2. Research self-publishing platforms, like Kindle Direct Publishing and IngramSpark. Compare their features to

determine which fits your book best, or publish on both.
3. Purchase an ISBN. To receive a discount see appendix 1.
4. Choose a memorable, meaningful imprint title, and create an imprint logo.
5. Establish a separate checking account and credit card for your business. Use an accounting software such as QuickBooks.
6. Determine your book's keywords, Amazon categories, and BISAC codes.
7. Create a book cover and format your book's interior.
8. To learn the intricacies of self-publishing, take the course How to Publish a Professional-Looking Book at CIPA.Podia.com.
9. Copyright your book.
10. Set up your Amazon author profile.

Chapter 7 Action Steps

1. Recruit three to five beta readers to provide feedback on your manuscript.
2. Seek endorsements from well-known figures or industry professionals to boost credibility.
3. Create and post social media graphics of endorsement blurbs when the book is launched.
4. Mail print copies of your book to influencers, along with a well-crafted letter suggesting ways they can help promote your book.
5. Produce a video book trailer to post on your website and social media platforms.
6. Update your online presence on all your author profiles and social media bios to include information about the new book.

Expand Your Reach through Advanced Marketing Strategies 181

7. Assemble a book launch team to help promote the book, provide reviews, and boost initial sales.
8. Schedule guest blogs and paid blogging tours to generate reviews and increase your book's visibility.
9. Write a press release and send it to local and regional media outlets.
10. Run Amazon ads to increase your book's visibility and sales.

Chapter 8 Action Steps

1. Send your edited and formatted book to editorial review sites months before its publication date.
2. Try to get ten book reviews during the book's formal launch week.
3. Ask for reviews when you give someone a book or receive positive feedback from a reader.
4. Continue to work on getting Amazon book reviews until you get fifty.
5. Send potential reviewers a clean Amazon book link.
6. Query book review bloggers to see if they would review your book on their blog.
7. Create an author profile on Goodreads and list all your books on this site.
8. Set up an author profile on BookBub. Investigate running a BookBub promotion.
9. Take the course Tips for Getting More Book Reviews on CIPA.Podia.com.
10. Request book reviews on book review sites.

Chapter 9 Action Steps

1. Create a calendar and budget for entering book contests.

2. Research reputable book contests and strategize which ones to enter within the first year of your book's publication.
3. Carefully review all contest guidelines and eligibility rules before submitting entries to avoid disqualification.
4. When attending a writers' conference, enter an unpublished manuscript, published book, article, etc. into their contest.
5. If you are a finalist, attend the award ceremony if possible.
6. After winning, attach the award emblem to your self-published book. If your book is published traditionally, buy the cover stickers to display on your books.
7. Update your author bio, website, and email signature with your award-winning credentials.
8. Prepare marketing materials and promotional graphics incorporating any award wins or finalist placings to post on social media.
9. Advertise your award-winning status on platforms like Amazon, Facebook, magazines, etc.
10. Write a press release about your win and submit it to local and regional newspapers and radio.

Chapter 10 Action Steps

1. Check out the Media Kit Guide, which reviews the ten essential ingredients to include in your media kit, at christianpublishers.net/free-gift. Assemble a professional media kit for each book or book series.
2. Produce a dedicated page on your author website to host the media kit digitally.
3. Create promotional materials such as book banners and bookmarks to attract attention at events. Schedule a bookstore event during the Christmas holiday season.

4. Download a printable version of a book marketing plan for you to complete at SusanUNeal.com/marketing.
5. Create a marketing plan listing each blog, magazine, and podcast you aim to pitch to. Based upon your personality, decide what type of marketing best fits you.
6. Consider whether setting up a Kickstarter campaign for your book would be beneficial.
7. Write guest blogs and articles for reputable websites and magazines to enhance your authority and improve SEO.
8. Plan a podcast and radio show tour that aligns with your book's theme.
9. Pursue television interviews by hiring a publicist or attending the National Religious Broadcasters Convention.
10. Track marketing efforts to measure their effectiveness and organize their links on an annual Word document.

Chapter 11 Action Steps

1. Develop digital products like books or checklists related to your book's subject to sell on your website.
2. Design courses that delve deeper into your book's content to engage and educate your audience.
3. Enhance your credibility by becoming certified in areas connected to your writing so you can offer professional services.
4. Start a speaking career to share your insights and sell books directly to attendees.
5. Organize or participate in online summits to gain exposure, network with other experts, and promote your products.
6. Become a book coach or editor to help others write their books.

7. Format books for authors using software like Vellum or Atticus.
8. Design book covers or book trailers for other authors.
9. Create a membership site where members can access exclusive content for a recurring fee.
10. Learn how to determine book categories and keywords for Amazon's advertising for other authors.

Chapter 12 Action Steps

1. Attend NRB with a booth. See appendix 1 for information about attending with CAN and CIPA.
2. Attend CPE with a booth so you can sell your book directly to retailers.
3. Rent a booth at a local homeschool convention if your book contains material helpful to homeschoolers.
4. Conduct school visits if you are a children's author.
5. Evaluate starting a podcast or radio show.
6. Consider launching a YouTube channel.
7. Seek divine guidance about creating a show.
8. Review all of this book's chapter action steps to determine which ones you will use.
9. Develop your comprehensive book marketing plan.
10. Implement your marketing plan.

Many techniques for marketing your Christian book exist—from getting Amazon reviews to winning awards. Just as you keep raising your child after they are born, you need to continue marketing your book years after its release. Just as a snowball gets larger as you roll it in the snow, the more layers you add to your book marketing, the more your sales will grow. Your journey has just begun!

Summary

As you wrap up this chapter, you're equipped with an arsenal of advanced marketing strategies that go beyond the basics. The approaches outlined here—from attending major trade shows to embracing digital platforms—elevate your book's visibility and broaden your audience. Whether you choose to connect face-to-face at conventions or engage readers online through multimedia channels, each strategy opens new doors for your book's journey.

Remember, effective marketing is about more than just promoting; it's about connecting with your audience in meaningful ways. You want to serve your audience. As you implement these strategies, keep refining your approach based on what resonates with your readers and your personality. The goal is not just to increase sales but to build lasting relationships with your audience, turning casual readers into devoted fans.

With a comprehensive marketing plan in hand, you're well on your way to not only reaching but exceeding your book sales goals. Embrace your marketing plan, stay persistent, and watch as your efforts help your book thrive in a crowded marketplace.

As we conclude this book, remember your writing is not just a career—it's a ministry. Through the pages you pen and the messages you share, you serve a divine purpose that God has laid on your heart. Your efforts to refine your craft and reach a wider audience aren't just about book sales; they are about carrying God's word to those who need it most.

This book has equipped you with the tools you need to manage and expand your ministry, enabling you to touch lives and make a meaningful impact. Stand firm in your calling, rely on the strength God provides, and move forward with confidence, knowing that your work fulfills a higher purpose in his grand design.

Appendix I: Author Resources

ProWritingAid Discount

Christian Indie Publishing Association (CIPA) members receive $150 off a lifetime membership with ProWritingAid at CIPA.Podia.com.

BookFunnel Discount

Christian Indie Publishing Association provides members with $50 off an annual BookFunnel membership at CIPA.Podia.com.

Lead Magnet and Email Marketing Course

CIPA members receive the courses How to Create a Lead Magnet: Start-to-Finish and Optimal Email Marketing, at CIPA.Podia.com.

Platform Building Course

Take the course 10 Steps to Building Your Author Platform, at CIPA.Podia.com.

How to Sell 1,000 Books in 3 Months Course

Take the course How to Sell 1,000 Books in 3 Months at CIPA.Podia.com.

Pinterest Course and Management

To learn how to manage Pinterest take the Grow Your Pinterest course or select Monthly Pinterest Management at TheBeautyOfTraveling.com/services.

Categories and Keywords Course

CIPA members receive the course Determine Your Book's Most Strategic Categories and Strongest Keywords, at CIPA.Podia.com.

Publisher Rocket Discount

Christian Indie Publishing Association provides members with a 30 percent discount on Publisher Rocket, at CIPA.Podia.com.

Book Category and Keyword Analysis

Susan Neal can determine your book's categories and keywords for you, at SusanUNeal.com/book-categories-and-keyword.

ISBN Discount

Christian Indie Publishing Association provides members with 10 percent off ISBNs from Bowkers, at CIPA.Podia.com.

How to Publish a Professional-Looking Book Checklist and Course

CIPA provides members with the checklist and course How to Publish a Professional-Looking Book, at CIPA.Podia.com.

Author Coaching

Susan Neal enjoys coaching authors through the self-publishing process and effective book marketing. Contact her for a free twenty-minute consultation at SusanUNeal.com/authorcoaching.

Book Contest List

Christian Indie Publishing Association provides members with an up-to-date list of book contests, at CIPA.Podia.com.

Book Metadata Checklist

Christian Indie Publishing Association provides members with a checklist of a book's metadata, at CIPA.Podia.com.

Amazon A+ Content

CIPA provides members with access to a graphic designer to create your book's Amazon A+ Content, at CIPA.Podia.com.

Press Release Guide

CIPA members receive the Press Release guide, which provides eight tips to craft a compelling press release, at CIPA.Podia.com.

Book Reviews Course and List of Book Reviewers

CIPA provides members with the course Tips for Getting More Book Reviews and a List of Book Reviewer Sites, at CIPA.Podia.com.

Book Launch Checklist

CIPA members get a Book Launch Marketing Checklist at CIPA.Podia.com.

Media Kit

CIPA provides members with access to a graphic designer to create your one-sheet or media kit, at CIPA.Podia.com.

Book Banner

CIPA provides members with access to a graphic designer to create your book banner, at CIPA.Podia.com.

Website Domain Authority Boost

CIPA provides members with access to a webmaster who

performs search engine optimization for websites, at CIPA.Podia.com.

List of 100 Radio & Podcast Media

Christian Indie Publishing Association provides members with a list of over 100 radio and podcast shows, at CIPA.Podia.com.

Marketing Tactic Worksheet

Christian Indie Publishing Association provides members with a Marketing Tactic Worksheet, at CIPA.Podia.com.

Media Query Tracking Sheet

Christian Indie Publishing Association provides members with a Media Query Tracking Sheet, at CIPA.Podia.com.

Trade Show Representation for NRB and CPE

CIPA provides members with the opportunity to attend two trade shows—NRB and CPE. See ChristianPublishers.net/tradeshows.

Annual Planning Course

CIPA members get an Annual Planning course, at CIPA.Podia.com.

Create & Sell Digital Products

Christian Indie Publishing Association provides members with the course Create & Sell Digital Products, at CIPA.Podia.com.

How to Create Amazon Ads Course

Christian Indie Publishing Association provides members with the Course: How to Create Amazon Ads, at CIPA.Podia.com.

Appendix 2: Editorial Resources

1. Christian Editor Connection at ChristianEditor.com/. Kathy Ide (KathyIde.com/) created this service, which personally connects authors with established, professional freelance editors who have been extensively screened and tested based on their specific genre and editing needs. Susan Neal recommends Kathy's book *Proofreading Secrets of Best-Selling Authors*. It improved her editing skills. Kathy has a book sequel, *Editing Secrets of Best-Selling Authors*.
2. Eva Marie Everson's editing services, Pen in Hand at EvaMarieEversonAuthor.com/contact. Eva Marie is the founder of Word-Weavers.com and is the Director of the Florida Christian Writers Conference and the Selah Awards.
3. Susan Neal's Christian nonfiction editor and book coach is Janis Whipple. Email her at JanisWhipple@gmail.com. Three of Susan's books Janis edited won first place in book contests.

Appendix 3: Certification Programs

1. American Association of Christian Counselors offers a range of certification programs, at aacc.net/.
2. The Advanced Writers and Speakers Association offers several certifications, at awsa.com/.
3. Christian Speakers Boot Camp offers a speaking certification, at RobynDykstra.com/inspirational-speaker-training/.

About the Author

Susan U. Neal RN, MBA, MHS, is a certified health and wellness coach dedicated to helping others enhance their health. Susan is the accomplished author of nine health-focused books, including the bestselling 7 *Steps to Get Off Sugar and Carbohydrates*, which won the Selah Award. Her most recent work, *12 Ways to Age Gracefully*, continues her mission to improve the well-being of the body of Christ, empowering them to serve God more effectively. She wrote, *Eat God's Food: A Kid's Guide to Healthy Eating* to educate children on healthy eating habits.

In addition to her wellness expertise, Susan is a certified writer coach, aiding fellow authors in publishing and marketing their own messages effectively. She won the Christian Author Network Excellence in Marketing Award for her exceptional promotional strategies. As the CEO of Christian Indie Publishing Association (CIPA), Christian Authors Network (CAN), Christian Indie Awards, CAN Marketing Awards, and director of the Blue Lake Christian Writers Conference, Susan plays a pivotal role in supporting Christian authors. Discover more about Susan and her work at Susan-UNeal.com.

Connect with Susan Online

Check out the Christian Indie Publishing Association blog which provides marketing, publishing, and writing tips at ChristianPublishers.net/blog/.

You can follow Susan on:
Bookbub.com/authors/susan-u-neal
Amazon.com/stores/Susan-Neal/author/B01FKRBXXU
Facebook.com/SusanUllrichNeal
Facebook.com/HealthyLivingSeries/
Youtube.com/c/SusanNealScriptureYoga/
Pinterest.com/SusanUNeal/
Instagram.com/healthylivingseries/
Linkedin.com/in/susannealyoga/
SusanUNeal.com
SusanNeal@bellsouth.net

Would You Leave a Review?

If *How to Sell 1,000 Books a Month* helped you in your author journey, would you please write a review on your favorite online bookstore? Your feedback not only blesses me, but it also helps other Christian authors discover this book.

Thank you for your support!
Susan Neal

facebook.com/SusanUllrichNeal
x.com/ChristianIndie2
instagram.com/healthylivingseries

Other Products by Susan U. Neal

All of the following products are available from SusanUNeal.com. The books are also available on Amazon at Amazon.com/stores/Susan-U-Neal/author/B07NWC7S42.

12 Ways to Age Gracefully

Though we keep adding birthdays, by making the right choices, we can look and feel younger. We may seek—and even pay a lot of money for—the newest anti-aging product. Yet the answers to gaining years of enjoyable life, and even looking younger, lie in our everyday choices. Through Susan Neal's own complicated health issues she learned the tools to move gracefully and joyfully through her senior years. Now she shares those tools with you!

7 Steps to Get Off Sugar and Carbohydrates

Over half of Americans live with a chronic illness and 42 percent suffer from obesity, primarily due to the overconsumption of sugar and refined carbohydrates. The faith-based book *7 Steps to Get Off Sugar and Carbohydrates* provides a day-by-day plan to wean your body off these addictive products and regain your health.

7 Steps to Reclaim Your Health and Optimal Weight Online Course

If you need additional support making this lifestyle change, purchase the course 7 Steps to Reclaim Your Health and Optimal Weight, where Susan walks you through the material covered in her Healthy Living Series. Learn the root causes of inappropriate eating habits to help you resolve those issues. Once solved, taming your appetite is much easier. Learn how to change your eating habits successfully once and for all.

Christian Study Guide for 7 Steps to Get Off Sugar and Carbohydrates

Struggling with health problems is not our true destiny. Many of the health problems we suffer are connected to eating habits. This study guide helps implement the plans in *7 Steps to Get Off Sugar and Carbohydrates*. Accountability and encouragement improve your chance for success. You only have one body, and you want it to carry you through this life gracefully. Reclaim the abundant life God wants you to live. Take this journey to recover your health with *Christian Study Guide for 7 Steps to Get Off Sugar and Carbohydrates*.

Healthy Living Journal

Have you tried to decrease your weight and improve your health without success? Or maybe you lost weight but gained it back. Don't allow frustration to take over. This journal will help you make and maintain healthy lifestyle changes.

During the next six weeks, commit to spend a few minutes daily recording your eating choices and how your body responds. With time you will see how different foods affect you physically and emotionally. As you record in this journal, you will begin to solve your personal health puzzle.

Healthy Living Series: 3 Books in 1

This megabook contains all three of the Healthy Living Series books:

7 Steps to Get Off Sugar and Carbohydrates

Christian Study Guide for 7 Steps to Get Off Sugar and Carbohydrates

Healthy Living Journal.

Solving the Gluten Puzzle

Are you experiencing symptoms that you or your doctor don't understand? Ruling out a gluten-related diagnosis may move you one step closer to wellness. *Solving the Gluten Puzzle* explains the symptoms, diagnostic tests, and treatment for gluten related ailments.

Eat God's Food: A Kid's Guide to Healthy Eating

Kids have strong opinions about food. Some foods they love and others they don't. Instead of letting their taste buds rule over your family's food choices, teach them early to love the right kinds of food. *Eat God's Food* teaches kids what foods are healthy and unhealthy, preparing them for a lifetime of eating and living the way God intended.

How to Prevent, Improve and Reverse Alzheimer's and Dementia

This pamphlet provides twenty-four interventions you can do to prevent, improve, or even reverse Alzheimer's and dementia. This is a synopsis of the study "Reversal of cognitive decline in Alzheimer's disease" by Dale E. Bredesen. The results of this scientific study is in understandable everyday language. Now there is finally hope. You can purchase this pamphlet at https://gumroad.com/l/mQNTE.

Scripture Yoga

Scripture Yoga assists yoga students in creating a Christian atmosphere for their classes. Check your poses with photographs of over sixty yoga postures taken on the sugar-white sands of the Emerald Coast of Florida. A detailed description of each pose is provided with full-page photographs so postures are easily seen and replicated. You can purchase these books at ChristianYoga.com/yoga-books-decks.

Yoga for Beginners

Yoga for Beginners eases you into the inner peace you long for at an easy, step-by-step beginner's pace. Through Susan's gentle encouragement, you will learn how to improve your flexibility and relieve stress. A broad range of yoga poses provides many options for the beginner- to intermediate-level student.

Made in United States
Orlando, FL
16 June 2025